Dr. Alan Ehler's role as dean and professo[r] [at ___ Univer]sity has put him in touch with thousands [of ___ around the] globe. He integrated what he has observed, [_____] and what he has learned from a large range [of academic] and practical sources into a fun read that can help you with the big decisions in your life.

> CAREY NIEUWHOF, founding pastor of Connexus Church
> and bestselling author of *Didn't See It Coming*

If you're like me, you may struggle with balancing various factors in decision-making. Drawing from multiple disciplines, Alan Ehler provides valuable insights for wise decision-making in this very readable book.

> CRAIG S. KEENER, F. M. and Ada Thompson professor
> of biblical studies, Asbury Theological Seminary

I know Alan Ehler and can speak with tremendous confidence that this book is not theory—this book is a way to live. In *How to Make Big Decisions Wisely*, Ehler lays out key principles for decision-making that integrate the findings of neuroscience, psychology, philosophy, and decision science with a biblical study of how the apostle Paul made decisions and directed those in the churches he founded to make decisions. This method works, and it will have a deep impact on your work and ministry.

> A. J. SWOBODA, professor, author, pastor

I had Alan Ehler as an instructor in my graduate program. He introduced Story-Shaping as a model not only for practical theology but also as a tool to be used in decision-making. It really helped me see the value of integrating intentional theology with the practice of my ministry. I am so very glad he is sharing this excellent concept with the world to help many others make good, godly decisions!

> HOLLY WAGNER, pastor at Oasis Church, author of
> *Find Your Brave*, and founder of She Rises

We all make big decisions from time to time, but how to do so wisely and in a way that fits with one's Christian vocation is an important issue. Alan Ehler's timely and insightful book provides a model for assisting Christians in their decision-making, both personally and professionally. It is rooted in Scripture and informed by science, making it a unique resource. I commend it most warmly to anyone who wants to know more about this important subject from a Christian perspective.

MARK J. CARTLEDGE, principal of London School of Theology

I have often heard it said, "First, you make the decision, and then that decision makes you." All of us have scars and successes to prove that adage true. Alan Ehler draws on years of experience and a lifetime of learning to bring fresh insight and key strategic steps to help us all make big choices wisely.

SCOTT R. JONES, senior pastor of Grace Church, Houston, Texas

I was encouraged by Dr Alan Ehler's book *How to Make Big Decisions Wisely*. The section on Story-Shaping was most helpful. I was amazed to look back on my life and see how closely the moves our family has made coincide with what he promotes in the book. Those who are in leadership at any level must approach this book as a must-read!

RICH WILKERSON SR., pastor of Trinity Church,
Miami, Florida, and author of *I Choose Honor*

Making major decisions is an unavoidable part of life. Every day we make thousands of remotely conscious choices ranging from trivial preferences to life-altering decisions, and few people are equipped with a framework to pass those conclusions through. In *How to Make Big Decisions Wisely*, Dr. Alan Ehler offers a clear and proven approach to help you make the kind of decisions that will lead to the best possible outcomes. I have benefitted from his wisdom in the classroom, and I believe this book will be a valuable resource to you.

TERRY M. CRIST, lead pastor of Hillsong
Church, Phoenix/Tucson/Las Vegas and host
of *Café Theology* on Hillsong Channel

HOW TO MAKE
BIG
DECISIONS
WISELY

A BIBLICAL & SCIENTIFIC GUIDE TO **HEALTHIER HABITS,**
LESS STRESS, A **BETTER CAREER,** AND MUCH MORE

ALAN EHLER

ZONDERVAN
REFLECTIVE

ZONDERVAN REFLECTIVE

How to Make Big Decisions Wisely
Copyright © 2020 by Alan Ehler

Requests for information should be addressed to:
Zondervan, *3900 Sparks Dr. SE, Grand Rapids, Michigan 49546*

ISBN 978-0-310-10650-0 (softcover)

ISBN 978-0-310-10652-4 (audio)

ISBN 978-0-310-10651-7 (ebook)

Published in cooperation with The Steve Laube Agency.

Cover design: Thinkpen Design
Cover photo: Voodoo Dot, An ku4ker/Shutterstock
Interior design: Kait Lamphere

Printed in the United States of America

19 20 21 22 23 24 25 26 /LSC/ 15 14 13 12 11 10 9 8 7 6 5 4 3 2 1

To Keira, who has helped shape all my
stories and made them much better

CONTENTS

PART 3: WHAT STORY SHAPING LOOKS LIKE

CHOICE AND CONSEQUENCES

I have set before you life and death,
blessings and curses. Now choose life,
so that you and your children might live.
Deuteronomy 30:19

We live or die by our choices, and no choice is innocent.
Take the simple act of picking out a piece of clothing. Choose a kilo (2.2 pounds) of cotton clothes—you have just chosen to use 29,000 kilograms (7,661 gallons) of water to grow it. Choose a kilo (2.2 pounds) of nylon—you have chosen to extract atopic acid from corncobs or oat hulls, which are grown anyway for food, so you haven't used any extra water. Choose a kilo (2.2 pounds) of rayon—and you have chosen to cut down trees, as rayon is derived from wood pulp. Every choice carries consequences.

So much of our lives is already chosen for us. Our parents. Our geography. Our economics. That's why every choice we make needs to be a wise one. How can we make better choices? Smart people don't always make smart choices. Alan Ehler has written a powerful book not just on "how to make big decisions wisely" but how to make every decision you make, even the smallest ones, count for good and for God, both for this earth and for eternity.

The connection Dr. Ehler makes between decision-making, "story-shaping," and health is as provocative as it is paramount. When William Tyndale published the first English translation of the New Testament translated directly from the Hebrew and Greek texts in 1526, he used the word *health* where we use *salvation*, which is itself derived from the medicinal word *salve*. The words for health, healing, wholeness, and holiness are basically the same. *Savior* is a healing word, and Jesus was a healer. Holiness is a "final integration" of mind, body, and spirit and the opening of connections between the human and divine.

I will cherish this book as a handbook on holiness and wholeness. The Latin root of the word *whole* is *totius*, which means both "to cure" and "to measure." For every living thing to be "well," there has a right "inward measure" that integrates the various parts into a functioning whole. When everything is in harmony, there is wellness and wholeness.

Those most ill may not have any physical problems. You can be physically fit and inwardly sick. The health of the spirit matters as much as the health of the body. Jesus died on the cross for our "salvation," to bring us into a "saving" state of health, holism, and holiness where our beings are metabolizing God's grace instead of guilt, grief, or despair and where our minds, bodies, and spirits are being wholly orchestrated by the Spirit.

We are more than the sum of our choices. But with each choice comes a consequence. And those consequences add up. This gem of a book will help you make life choices that have saving, healing consequences. The light of Christ, ignited by sparks flying out of this book, will come to new life within your soul.

Leonard Sweet,
Charles Wesley Distinguished Professor of Doctoral Studies,
Evangelical Seminary and Visiting Distinguished Professor
at Drew University, Portland Seminary, Tabor College

ACKNOWLEDGMENTS

I am overwhelmed with gratitude to many for their influence in my life that led to this book. I thank my youth pastor Randy Huddleston, who first led me to know Jesus personally. My parents, John and Gayle Ehler, have always modeled wisdom and fed my passion to learn and grow. My colleagues and my students at Southeastern University inspired me to take this model to a wider audience in prayer that it will help others too. My colleagues Sam Hemby, Bob Crosby, Ken Archer, and Brian Kelly reviewed an early draft and gave me excellent feedback. Len Sweet taught me to see the power of story and metaphor in embracing and communicating the work of Jesus and gave me the wording of Story Shaping. My agent Bob Hostettler is a big reason this book is here, and my editors Madison Trammel and Kim Tanner are the reason it is as good as it is. Thousands of other precious people come to mind from the churches where we worshiped and served together, the schools where we learned together, the miles we rode together, and the joys and tears we shared together. Thank you for sharing your stories with me.

PART
ONE

CHOOSING
WELL

CHAPTER ONE

THE CHALLENGE AND OPPORTUNITY OF BIG DECISIONS

How do you make big decisions? What do you do at those times when you know a lot is at stake? Making a bad decision can cost a lot. Making no decision can cost even more.

Think through your life. Can you see what an impact the decisions you made have had?

I was a senior in college at Rose-Hulman Institute of Technology, which was an all-male engineering school at the time. As a leader in its Air Force ROTC detachment, I would sit at the head table at our end of the year banquet, and it was just not cool to be there without a date. That made it decision time for me. I had no girlfriend, and there were no eligible candidates on my campus, so I had to decide what to do. I made a list of all the Christian girls I knew in the area and thought through each candidate using a variety of criteria: 1) commitment to Christ, 2) spiritual maturity, 3) ministry calling or compatibility, 4) personality, and, yes, 5) attractiveness too. One name emerged at the top of the list. A few conversations over the previous twelve months showed she was, indeed, fully committed to Jesus and his mission, she seemed one of the most engaging conversationalists I'd ever met, and she certainly met the last criteria too. The decision seemed obvious, but our relationship was not at a point that I had her phone number. Making that decision a reality would require action.

I knew I might see her if I visited a Campus Crusade for Christ (now called Cru) meeting at Indiana State University across town. Although it was my first visit to one of their gatherings, I knew many who were involved there. I found the meeting one Thursday evening, and as I entered and scanned the crowd, I saw my first choice dressed in a painter's outfit ready to rap the Four Spiritual Laws with some friends for Cru's yearly talent show.

When a break in the program came with an invitation to greet one another, I had to decide again to muster all the courage I could to go up to this painter-rapper and see if there might be some small chance she would speak to me. Of course, I feared rejection, but I decided to try anyway, and as I crossed the room toward her, she recognized me and gave me a great big smile that nearly launched my heart from its chest until she spoke and said, "Hi, Randy!"

My name is Alan. I still have not figured out who Randy is. And I thought her name was Kara—not the Keira her parents named her. Fortunately, we got the name issues resolved quickly, and Keira invited me to join her and some of her friends at the Campus Cupboard after the meeting. We talked for a couple of hours and found we shared much in common, most importantly, a love for Jesus and a passion to see him change lives like he had ours. I walked her back to her dorm and made another decision. I asked if she would join me at the banquet. It was then her turn to decide and she said yes.

Less than a year later, it was time to decide again. Thousands of miles of separation had not kept our hearts apart. We decided the rest of our lives would be better spent together than not, and now, decades later, I would not trade anything for the growing, deepening love, friendship, and ministry partnership we have enjoyed. What if I had picked another name on the list? What if I had chosen to go stag to the banquet? My life would be completely different today.

I am sure you can think of many decisions that have shaped your own life's story, but how do you make big decisions?

Big decisions shape the course of life. Choosing a major in college opens certain career opportunities and closes others. Marriage shapes both spouses. The job you take, the house you buy, the church you join, the ministry you launch, the business you start—these each set a course for a completely different life than if you had made a different decision.

Many people find themselves paralyzed by big decisions because so much is at stake. It can be tempting to hold off on choosing because of the fear of making a wrong decision, but indecision results in lost opportunities. In fact, to make no decision is a decision, often a poor one.

Some people decide intuitively. They go with their gut, hoping they can trust their emotions. Yet quick decisions can produce disastrous outcomes. Others seek to gauge popular opinion or gather the advice of people they trust. Others will turn to horoscopes or fortune cookies, hoping to get some magical direction. Of course the Bible condemns these as divination. Some well-meaning Christians read the Old Testament story of Gideon and put out what they call "fleece," hoping to get some supernatural direction. Other people make pros and cons lists. Some people hire a consultant. Others just go with the first thing that comes to mind. Far too many let indecision trap them, causing them to miss many wonderful opportunities because they never decide.

There is a better way.

The goal of *How to Make Big Decisions Wisely* is to equip you to make the best decisions possible in every area of life.

It introduces a model for making decisions called *Story Shaping*. This model is built on a foundation of the teachings of the Holy Bible, framed by centuries of philosophical consideration, and filled in with the most recent findings of neuroscience, decision science, psychology, and practical theology. Yet the model is simple to grasp and put into practice in your life and work today. Even if you are not a Christian, Story Shaping can help you navigate the dilemmas you face, the conflicts you encounter, the organizations you lead, and the relationships you pursue. But it works best if God is involved. I pray you will invite the One who made you into your big decisions.

At its core, Story Shaping embraces the concept that your life is a story. Your story started when you were born, and it weaves together with the stories of others born before and after you. Although you cannot control many of the experiences in your story, you can control how you interpret those experiences and how you shape them into an overarching narrative. Your decisions alter the trajectory of your story—and ultimately the stories of others too. Story Shaping offers a process for making the best decisions—intentionally and positively.

The best stories always involve conflict. How long would you stay in a theater watching a movie that was predictable, with no conflict or difficulties for the main characters to resolve? You might ask for your money back because a movie—or any story—without conflict is boring. Yet when we face a challenge or dilemma, our perspective changes. The excitement we felt in a theater seat can switch to paralyzing fear. There is no Hollywood scriptwriter behind the scenes to guarantee a happy ending to our story.

I refer to a dilemma as a hard choice that doesn't have a clear best decision. Individuals, groups, corporations, and governments all face dilemmas. These can boil down to simple choices, such as where to take a family vacation, or involve weightier decisions, such as whether to accept a job offer, the complexity of determining how to improve a product line's sales, or deciding amid crisis whether to go to war or pursue a peace agreement.

Though we cannot know the future, we can make better decisions and deal more effectively with dilemmas as we come to understand our stories and how we can shape both our stories and the stories of others. Story Shaping is a four-step process. It is a prayerful process integrating Scripture, theological reflection, and skills derived from decision science and neuroscience to discover and make the best decisions possible amid life's uncertainties. It does not guarantee a perfect outcome every time, but it does yield intentional wisdom as you follow its accessible, systematic approach to making decisions.

Much of Story Shaping's framework is adapted from the field of practical theology and its core objective of discovering what God is already doing in particular situations and what he wants us, his people, to do as well. The framework integrates biblical and theological wisdom to understand God, how he works, and how we can partner with him in his mission. Of course, decision making is a key element. Although practical theology's influence in seminaries is growing, it has yet to make a significant impact in the day-to-day lives of most people. Jerome Cottin writes that "the discipline of practical theology seeks to make connections between the various branches of social studies in and outside theology [to make it] a science for the contemporary world."[1] In other words, practical theology seeks to integrate theology with other areas of learning to provide practical help for churches and their people in today's world. That is exactly the objective of this book: to bring together biblical wisdom and the best scholarly insights to help you shape your story in the best way possible.

I use the word *story* in this book to describe the situations in which we, our friends, our families, our coworkers, our organizations, and even our societies find ourselves. A range of characters interact with us every day, affecting what happens to us. Events unfold like the plotline of a movie or novel. We are often in suspense, not knowing the outcomes.

Yet the difference in the story we live versus the ones we read about or watch is that we have some influence. This is why I call the model Story Shaping. "Shaping" implies some ability to determine what happens, though not the ability to control everything. No one can control a blizzard or hurricane heading toward your town. Yet you can prepare for it, and your preparation can make the difference between survival and destruction. The storm is the uncontrollable element, but your decisions shape the outcome amid the storm.

The term *Story Shaping* highlights the ongoing nature of circumstances. It can be tempting to view a situation as a one-time, stand-alone event. In reality, every situation is a product of the many events preceding it, and every decision will affect many events following it. Our lives are interconnected stories. A single decision can change your life and the lives of those around you.

Story Shaping provides a four-step framework for decision-making: (1) Read the Backstory, (2) Catch God's Story, (3) Craft a New Story, and (4) Tell the New Story. Following this process in your day-to-day life enables you to fulfill God's plan and experience God's grace as you make good decisions that benefit you, your church, your workplace, and the people around you.

The best stories are well told yet simple. They contain memorable characters who behave in an engaging manner to carry out a compelling plot. How we shape and live out our stories can make our lives more appealing, especially when other people are involved. Yet a continual process of evaluation and improvement is critical to keep our stories unfolding in the best way possible. That means multiple trips through the Story-Shaping process. Consider your car's engine. Every spark plug's explosion moves a piston around the circle only to fire again a thousand times a minute. The piston never moves beyond that circle, but your car does. The piston's cycle drives your car forward, and you cannot go anywhere without it. Just as engine cycles move a car forward on a long journey, continuing the Story-Shaping cycle can propel your life forward in increasingly better ways.

We all face big decisions. What dilemmas are you confronting right now? Will you be prepared when a storm hits? The Bible has a wonderful word for what it takes to make good decisions: *wisdom*. King Solomon told us wisdom is worth more than silver or gold. Proverbs 2:6 says, "The LORD gives wisdom," and James 1:5 tells us to ask him for it. My prayer is that God will use this book to give you more wisdom to make better big decisions and help you shape your story in the best way possible.

CHAPTER TWO

WHEN QUICK DECISIONS ARE BEST

Daniel Kahneman has researched the way people make decisions for over four decades. He and his partner, Amos Tversky, discovered that humans tend to default to one of two systems for decision making. What he calls System One is quick, automatic, and intuitive. System Two is slower, deliberate, and rational. His book *Thinking, Fast and Slow* lays out the implications of these two systems in a variety of settings. We tend to use System One far more often because it takes less effort. And many of our poor decisions stem from defaulting to System One instead of intentionally using System Two.[1]

Other research psychologists have observed similar behavior in a number of tests.[2] Their studies show that people tend to make quick decisions by defaulting to *heuristics*—rules of thumb, gut reactions, and other cues they have picked up—to decide as effectively as possible without expending much time or effort. Only when they view something as having sufficient value and uncertainty does it warrant intentional, reasoned processing.[3]

While Kahneman and others spend much of their time pointing out the flaws of using System One (fast-thinking) heuristics in decision making, most of the time it works well. Jonah Berger cites several psychological studies showing that people do better at tasks that are "automatic, natural, or well learned," but worse at tasks that are "more difficult or require more attention."[4] The pioneering American psychologist William James believed human brains are effective because we have "a far greater variety of impulses than any other lower animal."[5] The complexity of our own thinking means it would be difficult to accomplish much if we analytically processed every decision. John Kounios and Mark Beeman have conducted many studies of brain activity demonstrating that we use what they call mental "boxes" to simplify regular decisions and to make us more efficient.[6] In *Brain Changer*, David DiSalvo cites studies showing that a brain's "unconscious processing module" can handle about eleven million pieces of information per second. This information includes everything it takes to keep us alive, such as our breathing, heartbeat, cellular connections, hydration, digestion, and more. It would be impossible to do all that intentionally. Our "conscious processing system" can handle only about forty pieces of information per second.[7] The unconscious processing module handles 275,000 times as much.

Can you imagine waking up every morning by analyzing the noises you were hearing and going through an extensive decision-making process about whether to turn off your alarm? Once you had made that decision, you would need to go through another extensive process to decide whether to get out of bed. You would then have to spend another ten to fifteen minutes deciding which leg to stick out first. By the time the day was finished, you would be lucky to have finished breakfast.

I believe God intentionally designed us to have two processing systems. In *How We Decide*, Jonah Lehrer cites neuroscientific studies that have shown the intuitive and emotional region of the brain's ability to learn to function automatically and make quick decisions without intentional effort.[8] This ability is why professional athletes and musicians spend so much time rehearsing. When attacked by wild tigers, our ancestors did not have the liberty to take hours to analyze the situation. They had to act quickly to survive. Our Creator designed us to make most of our decisions quickly and intuitively so we can use the energy and resources required for intentional decision making when we face tough choices.

Although fast thinking and quick decisions have their place, they can also cause problems if we resort to them when a deliberate process like Story Shaping would prevent errors.

Kahneman provides several examples. For one, solve this problem:

A bat and ball together cost $1.10.
The bat costs one dollar more than the ball.
How much does the ball cost?

If you are like most people, the answer that first came to your mind was ten cents. But do the math and what do you discover? If the ball costs ten cents and the bat is one dollar more, the combined total is one dollar and twenty cents. Your fast-thinking intuitive brain fooled you.[9] It looks for cues to make quick decisions, but its method of judging and handling those cues cannot always be trusted.[10]

Neuroscientists have discovered that we use a particular region in our brains for fast thinking: the amygdala. Daniel Goleman points out how the amygdala connects to emotions and memories. Another region of the brain, the prefrontal cortex, conducts rational processing, what Kahneman calls System Two thinking. Goleman points out that strong emotions tend to activate the amygdala in what he calls "an amygdala hijacking," preventing us from accessing the more intentional prefrontal cortex—and System Two thinking—in highly emotional situations.[11]

Jonathan Haidt uses the metaphor of an elephant directed by a rider to explain the two ways people make decisions. The larger, stronger elephant represents the emotionally driven, intuitive system that can charge ahead without considering the wisest pathway. The rider mounted on top of the elephant represents the prefrontal cortex, our rationally driven, intentional system that carefully considers the best route to take. Just as it can be a challenge for a rider to control a willful elephant, our emotions often take over our decision-making unless we fight to regain control. Haidt and his coauthor Greg Lukianoff see this battle as one of the key challenges of this generation.[12] Will we let the elephant of emotion-driven, intuitive decision making run wild, or will we do the hard work of intentionally processing the decisions that really matter? Learning to use a method like Story Shaping can help keep our intuitive emotionally driven elephants under control.

STORY SHAPING

How can we know when to make intuitive decisions versus intentional decisions?[13] Often we have enough experience, wisdom, and training to trust our intuitive System One with a good, confident, quick decision—usually in familiar or predictable situations. This is the value of what Daniel Coyle calls *deep practice* and Malcolm Gladwell recognizes as the *Ten Thousand Hour Rule*.[14] When we work hard to develop a specific skill, we no longer need our slow intentional mental-processing system to complete the task. We can trust our intuition.

Here is a grid to pass any given choice through to determine whether you should apply Story Shaping:

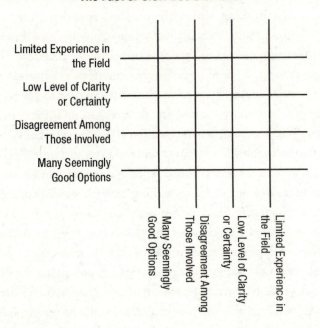

If an outcome is both uncertain and important, use Story Shaping. If you have little experience with the type of situation, if the key factors are unclear, if outside experts or others involved cannot agree on the right approach, or if there seem to be multiple options with equal chance of success, then an intentional decision-making process like Story Shaping is warranted.

However, if your choice can easily pass through the grid because the outcome is not highly important or you are confident you know what to do, then select one of the following fast-decision options:

1. **Do what the Bible says to do**—Christians have historically turned to the Bible as God's authoritative Word. It contains clear, applicable instruction for many things

we encounter. Should you cheat on your taxes to improve your financial situation? Romans 13:6–7 makes it clear the answer to that question is no. Should you help your neighbor in need during a tough situation? Matthew 5:42 and many other passages urge you to do so. When Scripture is clear and applicable to New Testament Christians, do what it says. A detailed decision process is not required.

2. **Do what has worked well in the past**—The old cliché makes sense: "If it ain't broke, don't fix it." Sometimes it is good to evaluate habits and systems to see whether we can improve them. But evaluation and improvement take time and energy that may be better spent elsewhere.

3. **Do what your training has taught you**—You may have taken courses, read a book, or learned from experience or from an expert about how best to tackle a dilemma you face. Airplane pilots go through hundreds of hours of training with instructors before they are allowed to fly solo. Reading books, listening to instruction, taking tests, and practicing with the instructor gives a pilot learned skills and habits that a pilot can trust will work every time. This can move the vast majority of decisions a pilot has to make into the fast intuitive category. Certainly, there are times to reevaluate our habits and methods of doing things to see if we can find a better way, but most of the time it is not worth the effort. You have learned what to do; you know how to do it well. Just do it as you were trained to do it.

4. **Go with your intuition**—As we saw above, God designed us to make most of our decisions intuitively. This approach usually is fine. You have developed skills and wisdom that can be trusted. As Emily Freeman says, do the next right thing.[15] This is an especially good way to go when not

a lot is at stake, but it does not always produce the best outcome. Several times I have noticed a traffic jam on the freeway ahead of me just before I got to an interchange and I did not have Google Maps, Waze, or MapQuest open. I had to choose quickly, and my only choice was to go with my gut. Sometimes those decisions saved me a lot of time. Many times they cost me hours in unnecessary back-road detours. If I knew all the side roads and traffic patterns, my success rate increased, but even then my intuition did not magically know everything about those situations. Yet unless I missed an important appointment, the risk was not too costly, and going with my intuition was fine.

5. **Do what you want to do as long as it does not violate your ethics and values**—If your motives are pure, you may often simply do what you want to do. Psalm 37:4 contains a wonderful promise: "Take delight in the LORD, and he will give you the desires of your heart."

Relying on quick thinking for the majority of our activities sets us free to reserve deliberate thought processes for creativity, planning, and problem solving. So do not waste time and effort on the easy stuff, but do not risk a bad decision by skipping the intentional process when you need it. Use the grid above to see whether your decision warrants Story Shaping. If so, read on to see how to put it to work. But before we get started with Story Shaping, we must answer some important questions.

CHAPTER THREE

HOW THE APOSTLE PAUL DECIDED

Will God give us specific guidance for every decision we face? This is an important question. If I say, "Jesus Christ is my Lord," that means he is my Master, and this confession means I am committed to do what he wants me to do. Therefore, I need to know what he wants me to do. How can I? Does Jesus tell us what he wants us to do in specific situations?

I will never forget being a young Christian and getting to know people at a new church. One woman in particular sprinkled nearly every conversation with the phrase "The Lord told me . . ." I was intrigued but also disappointed, as I was not experiencing this regular hotline from God. Over time, I learned that people have differing opinions on whether we can expect to hear from God outside of the Bible.

Some deny God has spoken since the New Testament was completed. Influential theologian and founding editor of *Christianity Today*, Carl Henry, wrote, "The Holy Spirit conveys no new truth." He argued that the Holy Spirit only illuminates and interprets the revelation already given in the pages of the Bible.[1] Similarly, Garry Friesen and J. Robin Maxson, say, "The Bible is fully sufficient to provide all the guidance needed for a believer to know and do God's will."[2] Kevin DeYoung claims, "The Scriptures contain everything we need for knowledge of salvation and godly living. We don't need any new revelation from heaven."[3] DeYoung's book *Just Do Something* features an alternate subtitle that sums up this perspective: *How to Make a Decision without Dreams, Visions, Fleeces, Impressions, Open Doors, Random Bible Verses, Casting Lots, Liver Shivers, Writing in the Sky, Etc.*[4] In that book, he writes, "Expecting God to reveal some hidden will of direction is an invitation to disappointment and indecision. Waiting for God's will of direction is a mess."[5]

If these were the only Bible scholars, it would be easy to assume special revelation is not an option today. Yet many theologians argue that specific direction from God can still happen. Paul Tillich wrote, "Christianity . . . should affirm that there is continuous revelation in the history of the church."[6] Richard Niebuhr wrote, "The God who revealed Himself continues to reveal Himself."[7] Dallas Willard was even clearer in his expectation of divine guidance: "There is no foundation in Scripture, in reason, or in the nature of things why any or all of these types of experiences might not be used by God today to communicate with his creatures."[8] German theologian Karl Barth believed the Holy Spirit enables all Christians to have their own personal participation in revelation from God, which gives us instruction and guidance we cannot receive any other way.[9] Barth wrote, "The objective possibility of revelation becomes a subjective reality."[10] Early Pentecostal scholar Stanley Frodsham stated this view succinctly, "Is it possible to be led by the Spirit of God every day in the year, every hour of the day, and every moment of every hour? Most assuredly."[11]

With such a split between Christian thinkers on this critical question, how can we find an answer? As Christians we turn to the Bible first for clarity. There we find in the apostle Paul's life a unique opportunity to study the Bible's principles of decision making, because we have both his own accounts of how he made decisions and how he wanted churches and leaders to make decisions, as well as the observations of his traveling companion Luke about his decision making, recorded in *The Acts of the Apostles*.[12]

If a Christian ought to rely on supernatural divine direction for every decision, we would expect to see Paul making his decisions on the basis of specific supernatural revelation from God and telling the churches to do the same. On the other hand, if God does not speak beyond the Scriptures, the book of Acts and Paul's letters would show decision making from natural, human reasoning in every case. I have studied Paul's life and instructions and have found several key principles on decision making.

1. God often gave Paul supernatural revelation.

    A supernatural encounter with Christ while he was on his way to arrest Christians in Damascus changed the course of Paul's life (Acts 9:1–19). His conversion was not a reasoned, intellectual decision. Jesus knocked him off his horse, spoke to him, and blinded him, and Paul was never the same. Although he never saw a blinding light again, the Bible tells us that God guided Paul several times through prophecy,[13] visions,[14] and an internal conviction of God's direction (Acts 19:21; 21:10–14).

2. Paul did not make most of his decisions through divine guidance.

    Although Paul experienced several instances of spectacular divine guidance, it seems Paul more often used his mind to make decisions. Luke was specific when describing Paul's decisions throughout Acts. Words such as decided,[15] resolved (1 Corinthians 2:2), chose (Acts 15:22

and 40), wanted (Acts 16:2), appointed (Acts 15:2), and judgment (1 Corinthians 7:40) show that Paul in most cases did not wait for a word from God before deciding. In Acts, Luke noted when supernatural direction occurred, and it is absent on the frequent occasions when Paul and his companions had to depend simply on wisdom and human reasoning.[16]

On Paul's first brief trip to Ephesus in Acts 18, the Jews there urged him to stay longer, but Paul responded with a phrase that Christians throughout history have used to connote the uncertainty of our earthly future: "If it is God's will . . ." (Acts 18:21). Paul used this phrase several times in his letters, Peter used it in his first epistle, and James urged his readers to use it on a regular basis in place of confident assertions of the future.[17] These words convey a truth that God knows and controls the future, but that first word *if* also shows us that we humans do not get to know everything about it. If mature Christians could know everything God knows, we would not need this phrase, but even the apostle Paul did not claim to know whether God wanted him to return to Ephesus, let alone what was the best choice in most decisions he faced. He had to rely on human wisdom instead.

3. Supernatural divine guidance most often gave Paul his main mission and objectives, but Paul usually made his own decisions about how to carry out that mission.

Jesus first appeared to Paul on the road to Damascus and gave him his life's mission statement: "I am sending you to them to open their eyes and turn them from darkness to light, and from the power of Satan to God, so that they may receive forgiveness of sins and a place among those who are sanctified by faith in me."[18] Paul did not need specific direction every day because his overall mission was clear. But God did speak at specific times and in specific ways to redirect how Paul carried out that mission.

Antioch had a strong church with both Jewish and Gentile Christians, but that church did not start planting churches in other cities until the Holy Spirit spoke through prophets to set aside Paul and Barnabas for missions that sent them around the eastern Mediterranean region and changed the course of Christian history (Acts 13:1–4). Luke rarely records the Holy Spirit telling Paul where to stop on his journeys. Those messages occurred only when God wanted Paul to change his ministry strategy.[19]

4. Paul expected the Holy Spirit to speak to Christians in a variety of ways.

Paul mentions a variety of spiritual gifts in his letters that enabled people to receive divine direction, including prophecy, speaking in tongues with interpretation, visions, dreams, and revelations (see Acts 2:17–18; Romans 12:6; 1 Corinthians 12:8–10; 14:1–40). In his first letter to the church in Thessalonica, Paul gave specific instructions on how to handle Holy Spirit–inspired messages, indicating an expectation that the Spirit would speak through ordinary people of the church unless they quenched the Spirit and held prophecies in contempt (1 Thessalonians 5:19–21). Therefore, it is clear that God spoke to the churches as well as to the apostles.

5. Paul expected the churches to make decisions using his instructions and wisdom more often than relying on divine guidance.

Paul's letters provide instructions to deal with specific issues and general principles for living as Christians in an unbelieving world, but Paul rarely told his readers to seek their own divine direction. Paul was clear about the character traits church leaders needed to possess, but being led by the Holy Spirit or having regular visions of Christ are not on those lists (1 Timothy 3:1–13 and Titus 1:6–9). Paul did not give instructions on how to hear the voice of God in any of his letters. He expected Timothy and all of those in the churches he planted to use their spiritual gifts, and he pointed primarily to his written instructions and earlier teaching to guide their actions and ministry (2 Timothy 2:2).

6. Divine guidance was corporate and interdependent far more often than individually given.

   Many instances of supernatural divine guidance required more than one believer to participate.[20] Prophecy was a regular occurrence in the early church, but when it occurred, the Holy Spirit would speak through one person to give a message to others. Similarly, Paul said the gift of speaking in tongues needed the gift of interpretation to be of value to the church (1 Corinthians 14:5–19). At least two people had to speak for others to understand the message. The Holy Spirit gave a gift to a person to benefit others, not just to benefit the individual who received the gift. Paul wrote, "To each one the manifestation of the Spirit is given for the common good" (1 Corinthians 12:7). Even Paul's encounter with Jesus on the road to Damascus was not complete until another man, Ananias, prayed for Paul to regain his sight and receive the Holy Spirit, and then gave him instructions from Jesus regarding his new mission (Acts 9:9–19; 22:12–16). It seems God most often spoke through one Christian to another rather than directly to the person.

7. Paul and the early church often made decisions through human wisdom in partnership with the Holy Spirit.

   There was not always a clear line between human wisdom and divine direction in Paul's life. Acts 15 provides one of several examples of this. Some Jewish Christians told Gentiles they needed to become fully Jewish to be saved, even getting circumcised. Paul and most in Antioch disagreed, believing that Christ's death and resurrection set all people free from such actions representing the Jewish Law. Leaders from both sides met in Jerusalem to work it out. Once everything was resolved, they chose to send a letter to the churches with the significant words, "*It seemed good to the Holy Spirit and to us* not to burden you with anything beyond the following requirements" (Acts 15:28, italics added). This sentence shows God's Spirit was at work in a group of Christians reasoning—and even debating—together. Note that God did not provide a clear, supernatural answer to the question at the beginning. It took work and some emotional exchanges to get to the place where participants could say they had found the Holy Spirit's answer, but they recognized he had been at work in the process.

   This partnership of divine providence and human effort may be a mystery, but it is clearly biblical. We must do our part. We are responsible for our own decisions and actions, yet God is often at work while we work.

8. Well-meaning, Holy Spirit–filled Christians occasionally disagreed on what they thought was God's will.

   The first part of Acts 15 shows the leaders of the early church working to resolve what could have become the first church split in history, but that chapter concludes with a split between two longtime coworkers and friends.

Barnabas wanted to take John (also called Mark) on their next missionary journey, but Paul did not want to take him because he had left them early on the first trip. If God revealed his will to his faithful followers on every occasion, why did these two—both apostles (Acts 14:14)—disagree so vehemently? Paul had grounds to question the wisdom of taking John Mark on the trip again. Barnabas tended to invest in those who had been rejected. He was one of the first to give Paul a chance, and Barnabas's investment in John Mark would eventually pay off. In the last chapter of Paul's final letter, he urged Timothy, "Get Mark and bring him with you, because he is helpful to me in my ministry" (2 Timothy 4:11). If divine direction were easy to obtain and available to every Christian for every decision, why has division so often polluted Christian history?

9. The Holy Spirit still provides guidance to Christians today as he chooses.

In 1 Corinthians 13, Paul wrote: "Where there are prophecies, they will cease; where there are tongues, they will be stilled" (v. 8). Paul explicitly states here that two of the ways God supernaturally communicated to the early church would cease. If the paragraph ended there, we could reasonably say that prophecy and speaking in tongues with interpretation were spiritual gifts the Holy Spirit gave for only a brief season in the church's history. But that is not how the paragraph ends. "Where there is knowledge, it will pass away. For we know in part and we prophesy in part, but when completeness comes, what is in part disappears" (vv. 8–10). Knowledge has not yet passed away. Some might say Paul's use of the word "knowledge" refers to the spiritual gift that he called the "message of knowledge" in the previous chapter (1 Corinthians 12:8).

Either way, if the completed New Testament is the perfect "completeness" Paul refers to in 13:10, it could make sense that verbal spiritual gifts would no longer be necessary. We have the Bible. Why do we need anything else?

The problem with this interpretation is that Paul was not equating "completeness" to the New Testament. Let's keep reading. "When I was a child, I talked like a child, I thought like a child, I reasoned like a child. When I became a man, I put the ways of childhood behind me. For now we see only a reflection as in a mirror; then we shall see face to face. Now I know in part; then I shall know fully, even as I am fully known" (vv. 11–12).

The completed New Testament gave the early church and the Christian church through all ages a much clearer picture of Jesus, his work on our behalf, and his plan for us. Yet none of us can say, "We know fully even as we are fully known." That day has not yet come. It will come when Jesus returns, but we are not there yet (see Colossians 3:2–4 and 1 John 3:2). Since that is the case and "completeness" cannot refer to the completed New Testament, there is no reason to assume the Holy Spirit has stopped gifting people in ways that enable them to speak for him at his initiative (1 Corinthians 12:11).

Paul's words to Timothy, "Fan into flame the gift of God, which is in you by the laying on of my hands" (2 Timothy 1:6), are similar to 1 Thessalonians 5:19–20 and indicate that if we do not earnestly use the spiritual gifts we have received, they are liable to lose their vitality and regularity. Perhaps lack of use is why some gifts of the Holy Spirit were absent from the regular experience of the Christian church through most of its history until the beginning of the twentieth century.

In summary, in Paul's life and ministry, revelation not only came to him but also to other leaders and ordinary lay Christians. Nothing in his writings or in the book of Acts suggests that supernatural guidance could not occur in our generation. Yet, like Paul, Christians today should not expect a message from God for every decision. Although Paul prayed for the Holy Spirit to give wisdom and revelation to other believers (Ephesians 1:17–19, Philippians 1:9–20, and Colossians 1:9), he also gave them practical instructions and never directed them to wait for special revelation to make a decision.

What this means for us is that God still speaks through special revelation, but not always. We need to make decisions in a manner that allows us to hear from God when he chooses to speak supernaturally, while relying on applied wisdom and biblical principles the rest of the time. Before we discover such a model, we need to learn to use an important tool.

CHAPTER **FOUR**

OUR STORY-READING GLASSES

We understand the world around us and how it operates by adopting stories, often called *narratives*. As my friend and colleague Ken Archer has written, "Story is the only way we can explain the meaning of our existence in a coherent manner."[1] Yet we may not recognize the stories we have developed to understand the world, our place in it, and why we do what we do. To understand them and the stories of others, we must first interpret them. It's not too different from how our five senses gather information and send it to the brain to be interpreted. For example, our eyes may see a long, narrow, slightly bent yellow object on the counter. Our hands feel that it is smooth. We peel open one end, take a bite, taste a distinctive slightly sweet flavor, and our brain says, "This is a banana!" Most of us would correctly identify the banana through sight alone, but even that is interpretive. Reading this page requires your eyes to see letters and your brain to interpret their meaning. Without the literacy training to recognize each letter, they would be meaningless squiggly lines.

How often do you consciously think about your eyes during a given day? You use them hour after hour but may not think about them. Because of my astigmatism and nearsightedness, if I do not wear contact lenses or eyeglasses, the world looks blurry to me. Once I wear the right corrective lenses, the world becomes clear. If I had never worn contact lenses or glasses, I would not realize what the world actually looks like. I might not have known that what I saw did not match reality. I may have assumed that everyone saw things the way I saw them—blurry.

When I wear contact lenses on a sunny day, I can put sunglasses on as well to diminish the glare. My clarity of view does not change, but the coloring of the world does. Ultimately, no matter what external lenses I wear over my eyes, each eye has an internal lens of its own. I am not usually aware of my natural lenses, but I would not be able to see anything without them. When I am outside on a sunny day, I can look through three lenses: my natural lens, which is part of my eye; my contact lens; and my sunglass lens. Each plays a different role in allowing me to understand the world around me. Yet I am actually using more than three lenses to understand the world. Each of my eyes has its own lens, and since my eyes see differently, each contact lens has a different prescription.

Whether you use prescription eyeglasses or not, you too use a variety of lenses to help you make sense of the world. I will refer to "lenses" throughout this book as a way to describe how people view the world differently and have different ideas about what is right and wrong, which leads them to make different decisions. Just like the glasses your grandfather may have put on to read a story to you from a book, these lenses filter our perception of the stories of our lives, and we've received them from our families, our education, our religious training, our experiences, our thoughts and reflections, the media, our friends, and a variety of other sources.[2]

I picture a set of reading glasses that consists of two lenses, each with four layers. The left lens (LL) represents things we consider intentionally: our beliefs, ethics, values, and reason.[3]

The right lens (RL) represents our "thinking without thinking" impulses: desires, instincts, skills, and habits. As we saw in chapter 2, God has equipped us with two ways to think and decide. One is slow and requires our intentional, conscious mental processing. This relates to the left lens (LL). The other way we think and decide is fast, intuitive, and usually unconscious. This relates to the right lens (RL).

Intuitive
1. Desire
2. Insincts
3. Skills
4. Habits

Intentional
1. Beliefs
2. Ethics
3. Values
4. Reason

THE LEFT (INTENTIONAL) LENS

Our intentions are key to making big decisions through Story Shaping, so let us look at each of the intentional lens layers first.

Left Lens Layer One: Beliefs

Intentional
1. Beliefs

Whether you consider yourself a Christian, a Muslim, an agnostic, or an atheist, you have beliefs. Beliefs answer the questions "What is?" and "What is not?" as well as "How do things work?" Beliefs include answers to big cosmic questions of how the world came into existence and what our individual place in the world is, but beliefs also include basic day-to-day functions of every area of life. Beliefs extend into anything we accept as reality. Do you believe that gravity will cause a rock dropped from a tree branch to fall to the earth? That is a belief. Beliefs vary among cultures and religious systems, but also among families and individuals. Beliefs can come from religious training, our parents, our education, our peers, our own experiences, and the media. Our beliefs can change, and some will change often, but they tend not to change as often or as quickly as other lens layers. But our beliefs do greatly impact the other layers.

Here are several examples of beliefs an American adult named Joe Jones may hold:

- I am a person, distinctly superior to animal life.
- I am a son of John Jones.
- I was created on purpose.
- I am loved by my parents and my wife.
- If I show up to work and do what I am asked, the company I work for will pay me.
- If I do exceptional work, I will be promoted.
- I can earn enough money to provide for my family.
- If I pray, God will hear and likely answer my prayer if it is in line with his will.
- I owe much of my quality of life to my country and those who fought for it.
- If I board a plane, it will most likely get me to my destination.
- If I put gasoline in my car's gas tank, the engine will run.

This list could go on for many pages, but you get the idea. Here is the beginning of a list of beliefs for a woman we'll call Tammy Smith:

- I am a result of the random chance copulation of two other beings.
- Human beings and all mammals, reptiles, and insects came into existence as a result of random mutations over millions of years.
- The emotion called love is an evolutionarily beneficial way to attract beings to copulate to continue the expansion of the species.
- There is no god, so prayer and worship are a futile waste of time and effort.
- When a human dies, his or her existence ceases, and there is no afterlife.

Tammy and Joe live in the same world yet function under dissimilar explanations of how and why the world works. Whether in marriage, business, friendship, or other relationships, differences in beliefs can make communication challenging, as a basic understanding of reality differs. Our beliefs integrate intentional thinking about decisions with unintentionally adopted understandings of the world. They blend giant cosmological, dogmatic beliefs with simple understandings of our daily routines. Let us explore how more subtle beliefs affect our understanding, communication, and relationships with others.

Imagine a man named Tom. Tom has always believed that his emotional state is determined by his circumstances and how the people around him treat him. When cut off in traffic, Tom gets angry. When Tom does not do well in sports or work, he finds someone to blame. Tom enters into marriage with the expectation that his spouse will make him happy. He feels full of love for her at the wedding ceremony and on the honeymoon, but as the young couple returns home to the daily grind of everyday life, his new wife turns some of her attention to work, to chores, and to her own hobbies. Tom becomes angry and resentful because she is "not meeting his needs." Tom remains miserable. His beliefs need to be reexamined.

Contrast Tom with Sue, who believes emotions happen for a variety of reasons. Some are situational, but her body's chemistry and her expectations have more of an impact on how she feels. Her favorite cliché is, "Life is 10 percent what happens to me and 90 percent how I respond." Though she may become alarmed when dangerously cut off in traffic, she does not take the action personally. When she fails to be promoted or win her tennis match, she carefully evaluates her own performance and works to improve the next time. Although Sue loves her new husband, she does not see him as responsible for her happiness. She draws from her own reservoir of contentment and resolves to love her husband and work together to build realistic expectations of each other. She does not take his outbursts of anger personally if she knows he had a hard day at work or is dealing with a disappointing stock market performance. Because of their differing beliefs, Tom and Sue can have divergent emotions in the same situation.

Our beliefs have an enormous impact on our relationships and our performance at school and work. Stanford University professor of psychology Carol Dweck has researched success. She uses the term *mindset* rather than *belief*, but her research shows the power of our beliefs and how they affect our actions and our ability to find success and happiness. She has found two predominant mindsets among people: *fixed* and *growth*. People with a fixed mindset tend to view their abilities and intelligence as unchangeable. Those with a growth mindset see themselves and others as capable of learning and improving.[4] Fixed mindset people function with labels like "I am stupid; I cannot do this; my results will never change." A person with a growth mindset will say things like, "I did not do well this time, but if I get training and practice hard, I will do better next time." Story Shaping adopts a growth mindset. It recognizes the importance of human growth and potential. It offers a way of plotting a better personal story moving forward.

Our beliefs about ourselves, others, the world, and God influence what we do and why we do it, but they do not determine what we do. The other seven layers of our lenses play a significant role in our understanding and our decisions.

Left Lens Layer Two: Ethics

Intentional
2. Ethics

Many beliefs directly affect our second intentional layer— ethics. This lens answers the questions "What should and should not be?" and "What must and must not be?" For those whose belief lens layer is conservative Muslim, the Qur'an will determine much of their ethical lens layer, what they should do. Bible-believing Christians draw many of their *shoulds* and *musts* from the Bible. Citizens of a country may share a belief that we should all obey laws. But not all our ethics are as clear or grounded as we might think.

Tom, from our earlier story, believes other people and circumstances are responsible for his emotions. That belief can translate into a serious list of *shoulds* (in his mind) for anyone in a relationship with him. He may not use these exact words, but the following phrases could describe his thoughts about relationships:

"My wife should make me happy." "That car should get out of my way." "My boss should give me a raise." Note that the Toms in this world have a different set of ethics for others than they have for themselves. What happens when Tom's ethical standards are not met? He reacts with deep anger or sadness, especially when the ethics are of a *must* variety. A *must* is present when it is impossible to imagine life existing in the absence (or, in the case of a *must not*, the presence) of the "ethic."

Brenda has always been a clean freak. Her mother maintained a spotless household, and Brenda adopted the belief that cleanliness is next to godliness. She imagines any spot of food on the counter or floor will spread germs, harming her and her family. When Brenda's husband, friends, and children are not careful to clean up their messes, she reacts with fearful anger. "Our house *must* be clean! We *cannot* live in a mess!"

Like beliefs, ethics can come from our religious backgrounds and parents. But society and the media can influence people to change their ethics. The great eighteenth-century economist Adam Smith recognized how effective the new genre of the novel was in shaping the views of people in his day on interactions between classes, sexual morals, and the economics of inheritance.[5] Many studies show how movies, television, and news media have prompted Americans' acceptance of things formerly forbidden.[6] It would be tough to measure the full influence of Sidney Potier's memorable movie characters from the late 1940s through the 1960s in confronting the stigma of race for many Americans. Audiences can emotionally identify with characters who represent ethics they might have opposed before. This is the power of story. Vivid, emotional portrayals enable viewers to see through a character's eyes and understand the character's perspective. This can lead to a softening of "shoulds" and "musts." Watching R-rated movies may lead a teen from a strict no-drugs upbringing to question the ban on taking illicit drugs. What was a "must not" now becomes a "may," and one previously committed to staying drug-free now feels free to experiment. Peer pressure can have a similar effect on changing the ethics of individuals and groups. All these factors have shifted popular ethics—what most ordinary people believe is right and wrong—in societies around the world in recent decades. Yet we should be clear that Christians believe first in God-defined ethics that transcend those developed by any community or individual. The Bible is filled with clear commands that are not changed by shifts in popular ideas about what is right and what is wrong.

Left Lens Layer Three: Values

Intentional
3. Values

The third layer of the intentional lens includes the things individuals, groups, and societies care most about—their values. The intuitive right lens has a layer called desires that are distinct from values. These are immediate urges that may not reflect deeply held values. For example, Tanya values eating healthy and staying fit. But when a slice of freshly baked chocolate cheesecake is placed in front of her, she eats it, giving in to an intuitive desire.

Values vary from person to person. Our values are shaped by our families, education, media, peers, and religion. We draw many values directly from our ethics and beliefs. I value being known for honesty and integrity because I am a Christian and I try to derive my ethics from the Bible, which commands telling the truth. But I could hold that same value of integrity simply because I want people to trust me as a salesperson so I can make more sales. The source of my value and my motivation for holding that value are different, but the value remains the same.

Values can vary greatly among individuals who have similar ethics and beliefs. A difference in values can thus become a source of conflict between members of a family, business, or club. Early in our marriage, my wife and I discovered she valued doing things *well*, while I valued doing things *on time*. Ideally, we both want everything done well and on time, but when a choice must be made between the two, I would rather finish by the deadline, even if the result is not perfect. I got angry at being late, and she got angry at me for pestering her to accept a lack of excellence just to meet a deadline. It took several years for us to understand how this difference in a deeply held value could create such conflict between us.

Imagine the tension and conflict between individuals caused by a choice of differing values.

- Which do I care about most: my family, my country, my friends, or myself?
- Is career success and earning money more important than eating dinner with my family every night?
- Which environment do you prefer: a tightly controlled, structured, and secure environment, or freedom to do what you want even if it risks danger and violence?
- Which is more valuable: consistency or variety? Do I order the same entrée at the same restaurant every time I go out to eat, or do I go to a new restaurant and try something I have never eaten?
- Is work more important to me than recreation?

- Which is more important: to be polite or to tell people the truth even if it offends them?
- Do I choose to be generous to those in need, or do I want to see them become self-sufficient?

This list could go on indefinitely, but thinking about the tensions between values gives us a sense of how values affect our actions, which can create conflict with other people.

Academic psychologist Clare W. Graves, in the middle of the twentieth century, developed a theory he later termed Spiral Dynamics to explain how individuals and societies think and act, as well as how cultures have developed throughout history. He called it "emergent cyclical levels of existence theory." Graves's work was not published until he partnered with Don Beck near the end of his life in 1975. Beck systematized and popularized Graves's work, which went on to have tremendous influence on psychology, anthropology, and business.

One of the core concepts of Spiral Dynamics is the eight "value systems" that categorize societies. Beck and Graves determined that cultural conflicts often result from values systems conflicts. Beck was invited to South Africa by then-President Nelson Mandela to help the country navigate massive changes in the culture and values after the abolition of apartheid, with the goal of ending racism.[7]

While there have been challenges to aspects of Spiral Dynamics theory, what Beck and Graves's research revealed is how significant an individual's and a society's values are in influencing responses to crisis, conflict, and change. It also showed how values, in most cases, are closely linked with beliefs. This is why values is a critical layer in Story Shaping's intentional lens. Whether we want to improve a marriage, adapt our business to changing times, or foster relationships with our neighbors, it is helpful to first determine what we and others value so we can ensure those values are preserved as we move ahead. If I fear that the change means losing something of great value, I will not be eager to make that change. But if I am shown that something of greater value is risked by not changing or something better could be won by changing, I may be more willing to go ahead with the change.

Left Lens Layer Four: Reason

Intentional
4. Reason

The final layer of the intentional lens is "reason," the mental processing of new information and experiences and their implications. We use reason to determine whether a message we heard is true (in line with established facts) and good (in line with our own ethics). We can use reason to find any inconsistencies in another's statements. We also use reason to determine how opportunities, challenges, and the views of others align or don't align with our beliefs, ethics, and values. Reason can help us determine how to act and what to do, especially in complex situations. We consider a situation and ask ourselves: "What do I believe about what is going on?" "What do I think is the best choice?" "What should I do?" "What do I care about that is at stake in this decision?"

No one knows everything about everything, and, in many cases, we start with inaccurate information. Reason can be used to take in new information gleaned from reading, education, research, experience, or relationships. We might then adjust our beliefs, ethics, and values.

Nicolaus Copernicus's discovery that the sun is the center of our solar system provides an example. Copernicus was raised to believe the earth is the center of the universe. That was the story he lived by. His parents, teachers, priests, and peers generally accepted the story and reinforced it with him. But his astronomical observations, in conjunction with wide reading and study, convinced him that the geocentric theories held for centuries did not match reality. He observed and verified his alternative heliocentric theory for years, sharing it only with his closest friends, afraid of the criticism he would receive from other scientists, political leaders, and the Catholic Church. He had formed his theory by 1504, but he did not begin writing about it until 1514, and he did not complete the full statement of his theory in *De Revolutionibus Orbium Coelestium (On the Revolutions of the Heavenly Spheres)* until he was on his deathbed in 1543.

Copernicus's theories were groundbreaking. Many scientists accepted them, including Galileo Galilei, who was put on trial by church leaders who were unwilling to consider that their own geocentric story might be in error. The earth had always rotated around the sun, regardless of what anyone had thought. Yet it took careful observation to show how Western society had been in error, thinking the sun orbited the earth. Some still clung to the old story, and conflict erupted among those who held to the story of tradition and those whose story had been changed by science.

Reason aids in resolving conflict between differing stories. The stories of individuals often conflict. A conviction on one layer of a person's lens may be incompatible with a conviction on another layer. Sometimes the individual is unaware of the conflict. Other times the individual is very aware.

An example of the second type of conflict is a husband who holds the religious ethic that adultery is wrong yet surrenders to the impulse to have an affair with a coworker anyway. The guilt he experiences is a result of his awareness of the conflict between his ethics and his actions.

Awareness and guilt do not accompany all internal conflicts. Think of a person who values being a law-abiding citizen and holds to an ethic stating that it is wrong to break the law. One day, while driving on the highway, she fails to notice a sign dropping the speed limit from 60 to 35 miles per hour. She did not break the speed limit intentionally, yet her actions violated her ethics and values. We can be ignorant of an internal conflict.

Another example is what we call a "double standard," the person who is angry at someone who cuts him off in traffic, and angry at those who honk at him when he cuts them off. We say he has one ethic for himself and another for everyone else. In many cases, people are unaware of their double standards. A double standard can exist within the same layer of lenses, such as the angry driver above. Double standards can also lie on different layers, for example, valuing harmony in a family while holding an ethic that a parent must punish a child's wrongdoing, even if it provokes the child to lash out in anger, then run away from home. Harmony and justice cannot always coexist. Double standards like these are a cause of much frustration, discouragement, and depression.

Fortunately, our stories can change, and reason is usually a part of the process. Sometimes change happens on our own as we recognize conflict between our lens layers or between the story we hold and the reality around us. When we consider evidence that contradicts our story, we can change our story, refute the evidence, or deny its implications. Or another person may persuade us to change our story. It is difficult to remove the lenses we have looked through for years, even when they are inaccurate. Counselors, teachers, pastors, friends, and others can help in that process.

Story-Shaping reason has limitations, though. Some choose not to evaluate a conflict between experience and beliefs despite the evidence. Others cling to old ethics and values even when their belief systems change. This may be why some secular writers and speakers use absolute language ("This is wrong! That is right!") while denying the possibility of moral absolutes. They don't recognize how religious faith and its concept of objective ethics has influenced their own thinking.

Although we may assume reason always leads to truth, motives can cause two people evaluating the same evidence under the same circumstances to adopt different conclusions. Reason is not a perfectly pure layer of our intentional lens.

Nineteenth-century Danish philosopher Soren Kierkegaard wrote, "Human reason has boundaries," while arguing that most human decisions are not based on rational considerations but rather on "subjective meaning."[8] We act on our whims. Recent findings of neuroscience and decision science support Kierkegaard's conclusion. Most of our decisions use Kahneman's System One "fast thinking." Much of our outlook develops without any conscious effort. We need another lens to explain this intuitive aspect of how we see and understand the world and decide in response.

THE RIGHT (INTUITIVE) LENS

In the metaphor of the lenses I am using to explain how people understand the world and make decisions, the fast-thinking brain is called the "intuitive right lens" (RL). I use the word *intuitive* to imply that deliberate effort is not used. This lens has four layers that shape what we see and how we instinctively act.

Right Lens Layer One: Desires

Intuitive
1. Desire

Desires are emotional and physical urges to do something. Many of these are natural and essential parts of our human systems. If I am thirsty, I crave water. This is my body's way of warning me to drink water to avoid the debilitating effects of dehydration. My body lets me know I need to sleep by making me tired. But acting on some desires can be destructive. Striking your spouse in the middle of an argument is the result of a strong desire, but it does not build a healthy marriage. Fear is a powerful urge that can save life, but fear can also cut off our intentional thinking and our ability to reason (an example of "amygdala hijacking" mentioned earlier). Our more primitive brain can take over in an emotional crisis and prevent us from thinking intentionally and rationally.

Desires often run counter to our ethics and values. You value fitness and hold the ethic that healthy eating is important. You adopted this ethic after a visit to your doctor, who warned you that your health was not good. Before that visit, you valued the taste of food over its health benefits, but now your *reason* took in the doctor's warning and the evidence he provided, and you changed your beliefs, values, and ethics. Now you believe that how you eat affects the length and quality of your life, you value health over taste, and you have convinced yourself that you *should* eat healthy. That is your intentional lens doing what it should do.

Suppose you decide to visit your mother one week after starting a low-carb diet. You called first to see whether she was home, so she had time to bake a batch of your favorite homemade cinnamon rolls. You walk into her home already hungry and smell that unmistakable aroma of freshly baked cinnamon rolls, the tastiest on the planet. Your desire goes to work immediately. You want a cinnamon roll. The battle between the intentional side of the brain and the impulsive, intuitive side flares up immediately. It is not difficult to see the power of desire.

Right Lens Layer Two: Instincts

Intuitive
2. Insincts

Instincts are actions we do without thinking and without anyone teaching us how to do them. Breathing is a great example. You did not consciously learn how to breathe when leaving the womb, and I bet you did not consciously think about the breath you took before beginning this paragraph (although you might be thinking about it now). Most of our bodies' systems function without any conscious thought from us.

Instincts also include what we sense to be right or true without conscious consideration. This works well for us most of the time, but there are occasions when our instincts are not accurate. Kahneman provides examples from a variety of disciplines in which "experts trust their guts" with disastrous results. One is the "*Sports Illustrated* jinx." The world's leading sports magazine traditionally sought the "hottest" player in professional sports over the previous month and ran his or her photo on the magazine's cover, under the assumption that their hot streak would continue. Inevitably, the month after the issue, the player's performance would plummet. Kahneman does not believe in a cosmic curse or jinx, but rather a statistical regression to the mean. In other words, the streak was not a sudden improvement in that player's ability, but a statistical anomaly. The post-*SI* cover crash is simply the player returning to normal.[9] If while playing dice I roll doubles twice in a row, I may *instinctively feel* I will roll doubles again, but the odds are highly against it. Actually, the odds are the same every time I roll the dice (unless they are loaded).

Right Lens Layer Three: Skills

Intuitive
3. Skills

Skills are complex abilities we had to learn through intentional effort, but we can now do them without conscious consideration. Do you remember when you first learned to drive a car? You had to think about everything you did: what pedal to push, how hard to push, how far to turn the steering wheel, what mirror to use, how close to follow the car in front of you. Every action required constant, deliberate thought to get it right, and if you were like me, you occasionally did not get everything right. Now, if you have been driving for a few years, you do not even think about those things. Driving is a learned skill that your intuitive system can manage unless you find yourself in the midst of an ice storm or another tricky driving situation that forces you back into more intentional thought processes.

Intentional thinking requires time and energy. Once we are able to perform a task well without intentional thinking, we can do it much more quickly, with less use of energy, often resulting in a better outcome or product. Matthew B. Crawford uses the ancient mariner term "jigging" as an example of the efforts of an expert, one skilled in a certain task. Like a carpenter using a piece of wood of a specified length to serve as a guide for others, quality jigging sets apart the expert from one less skilled. Jigging, Crawford notes, also happens mentally: "Once we have achieved competence in a skill, we do not routinely rely on our powers of concentration and self-regulation—those higher-level executive functions that are easily exhausted. Rather, we find ways to recruit our surroundings for the sake of achieving our purposes with a minimum expenditure of these scarce mental resources."[10]

In *The Talent Code*, Daniel Coyle gives many examples of how exceptionally skilled people who appear to have an abundance of "talent" actually exercise skills learned through what he calls "deep practice." This practice is the intentional repetition of challenging activities until they become second nature. One who has reached a level of expertise does not need to invest time and mental energy in making decisions but can respond by instinct.[11] Similarly, in his book *Wait: The Art and Science of Delay*, Frank Partnoy cites studies which show that experts do better in situations requiring their expertise by using a practice he calls "sampling": choosing to react intuitively rather than taking time to process through a decision.[12]

I began bicycling seriously in 2006. My wife, Keira, soon joined me, and we found a good group to ride with in our community in the state of Washington. The next year we made a commitment to join ten thousand cyclists in the Group Health Seattle-to-Portland (STP) Ride. We rode over two hundred miles in one day and had a wonderful time. I had grown in my cycling skills during that first year and gotten the sport into my blood. I even started watching the Tour de France that month, imagining what it would be like to sprint across the finish line in first place.

Less than two weeks after the STP, Keira and I joined friends for what was to be a 65-mile ride along the western slopes of the Cascade Mountains. The last segment was the relatively flat and safe Centennial Trail. As we approached an intersection, I heard my cell phone ring in my pocket. I pulled it out and realized my son was calling. I told Keira and the rest of the group I would meet them at a rest stop less than half a mile ahead.

After I finished the call, put the phone in my back jersey pocket, and crossed the road, I decided to try sprinting down the trail like the Tour de France racers I had watched on TV. I stood up on my pedals and pounded on them with all the force I could muster. At least that is what I think happened. The world suddenly went dark. The next thing I saw was a blurry group of people standing over me asking questions I could not quite decipher. In fact, I was not sure I could answer any of their questions. I got out the only phrases I knew for sure: "My name is Alan, and I am married to Keira."

It took some time to heal from the double break in my collarbone, five broken ribs, and concussion resulting from that strange crash that probably resulted from hitting something on the trail that pushed me over the handlebars. After six weeks of recovery, I got back on the bike and worked to improve my skills. Seven years and nearly forty thousand miles later, I began riding with a group of friends near our new home in Florida. One day we rode a route with designated "sprint points" along the way, where we could compete to see who crossed the lines first. As we neared the fastest sprint point, I was in an excellent position to attack from a few bikes behind the leader. I stood to sprint with all my might. Suddenly, my chain caught in the front derailleur, and my pedals would not turn. With all that force coming on the next pedal stroke, I nearly tipped the bike over. That is not a fun prospect at 37 mph with twelve other aggressive cyclists hot on one's wheel. Had my skill level been what it was in 2007, I would have hit the pavement hard, and at least half a dozen cyclists would have ridden right over me and left plenty of their own skin on the tarmac that day.

But I had picked up a few skills in those forty thousand miles. The fraction of a second I had to react to the locked-up chain did not give me enough time to intentionally think through options. I acted without thinking, using learned skill, immediately compensating for the shift in balance. I slid off my seat and swung my body weight in the opposite direction. The front tire wiggled, and I slowed down a little (much to the dismay of the riders behind me, who hoped to ride my draft before sprinting past me at the line), but I stayed upright. A learned, now intuitive, skill prevented what would have been a sure crash.

Right Lens Layer Four: Habits

Intuitive
4. Habits

Habits are behaviors we developed at some point in our lives that have become routine. We now do them without thinking. For example, your mother may have regularly told you to turn off the lights when you left your room when you were three years old. She may have had to remind you several times a day then, but now you turn off the lights when leaving a room out of habit, without thinking about it.

In his book *The Power of Habit*, Charles Duhigg calls the habit-forming process "chunking." The brain converts a sequence of actions into an automatic routine as part of its ongoing effort to improve efficiency.[13] Duhigg refers to the process of developing a habit as the Habit Loop. The loop is triggered by a cue of some sort (perhaps a craving for something like a cigarette), which leads the person with the habit to begin the routine (often satisfying the craving), which then yields the reward (the good feeling that accompanies the behavior). You may have entered the Habit Loop intentionally the first time, but, before long, your brain passes through the loop on a regular basis without thinking in order to get that reward.[14] Many corporations in all types of fields, including food production, have discovered the power of habit and seek to facilitate addictions that produce the Habit Loop.[15]

As with so much of our intuitive thinking, some habits are good, some are destructive. We all know bad habits are hard to change. It takes intentional effort. One of the biggest challenges to changing habits lies in not fully accessing our intentional thinking. We need to learn the consequences of bad habits to change our beliefs about them. Yet belief change alone is rarely enough to produce habit change. Nearly every smoker has heard the warnings of lung cancer. Many even adopt the ethic that smoking is bad. The challenge is to adopt the *value* that says, I want to stop smoking more than I want the next cigarette. We must muster intentional will in full force to combat the combined effect of habit and desire. With smoking, chemical assistance such as Nicoderm and patches can help curb urges. In many cases, breaking bad habits requires analyzing several factors involved, such as time, freedom, relationships, identity, and fears that are associated with acting or not acting on the habit. Story Shaping can be an excellent process to work through habit change as well as many other types of positive change in your life.

By seeking to understand how we and others interpret situations through our intuitive and intentional lenses, we can head toward better decisions and conflict resolution. Our interpretive lenses are the source of most decisions we make, whether intentional or intuitive. God has designed our brains to do most of their work intuitively, allowing us to reserve time and energy for the challenging decisions that matter most. Therefore, the first step in Story Shaping is simply to ask whether we should use the process for a particular decision, as we saw in chapter 2. When we face a dilemma that our intuitive system is not equipped to handle, it is time to begin the intentional decision-making process of Story Shaping.

PART
TWO

STORY-SHAPING
STEPS

CHAPTER **FIVE**

STEP 1: READ THE BACKSTORY

Toyota dramatically changed its small, economical, boring family-car image in the mid-1980s with the release of the MR2 Roadster. The MR2 was a huge hit in Japan, winning "car of the year" in 1984, and in the US. But the MR2 had a completely different reception in France. Saying "M-R Deux" sounds an awful lot like the French word for defecation. Who wants to spend money on a car whose name means excrement?

In a similar story, Mercedes Benz expected great success from its new GST model, released around the world in the 2005 model year. The GST sold well everywhere except in Canada, where those three letters are the abbreviation of the ubiquitous and hated Goods and Services Tax.[1]

Misunderstandings and misinterpretations go far beyond translation challenges. Every human has a unique set of experiences. Parents raise children differently, even children in the same family. Variations in culture and education, even subtle ones, can greatly impact how we view the world, other people, and why things happen.

This first step of Story Shaping—Reading the Backstory—helps us understand what is currently happening in our lives and why. With chronic, recurring problems, learning more about the stories of those involved can often lead to a diagnosis of the real source of the trouble. Whatever dilemma you may face, you are more likely to make a better decision if you understand the real story, rather than just seeing what's on the surface.

Imagine you install a concrete patio behind your house. A week or so later, you notice a crack starting to form, and it looks ugly. Your concern may be about the appearance. A seemingly easy fix is to get some concrete patching compound, mix it with water, and wipe over the cracks. That can fix the appearance for a day or two, or perhaps even a year, but you did not discover the real story.

Before getting into vocational ministry, I was a civil engineer in the US Air Force. In my college days, we learned the properties of concrete. As it cures, concrete's molecules pull together, which causes the hardening compound to crack. Sidewalks and concrete roads have joints to control where this cracking occurs. Perhaps your patio slab is too large, and an intentionally placed contraction joint would have prevented the unsightly, irregular cracking. Although ugly, these kinds of cracks do not pose a structural risk. There could also be a structural reason for the cracking. Perhaps the soil and gravel under the slab were not adequately compacted. Over time, your patio may begin to shift, with one side of the crack rising higher than the other. In that case, your patchwork will crack and become even uglier. Depending on where you live, these cracks could even be a sign of a sinkhole forming. If so, you would be in real trouble that no amount of patching could solve.

In much the same way, not taking the effort to read the backstory in any situation you face may result in a futile attempt to patch a problem that requires a different solution. Understanding the stories of others helps to improve relationships. The apostle Peter instructs husbands to "be considerate as you live with your wives" (1 Peter 3:7). Too many marital conflicts result from viewing a situation from one's own perspective without taking time to understand how one's spouse views it. A lack of understanding of others' perspectives is a root cause of many conflicts. The Philippian church included members who had a disagreement, so the apostle Paul called on them to become "like-minded" and "not looking to [their] own interests, but each of you to the interests of the others" (Philippians 2:1–4). We each have had experiences and lessons throughout our lives that molded our unique outlook. This is what makes relationships fascinating and compelling, but it is also what makes them challenging.

As we saw in chapter 1, we each use different *stories* to understand and explain the world and our role in it. Story differences are the source of many of the world's conflicts. Failing to understand other people's values or beliefs before entering into agreements has caused an untold number of problems for governments, corporations, and families. This is why Story Shaping begins with reading the backstory.[2] This step encompasses seeing what is happening and why, then determining what is helpful and should be retained as well as what should be eliminated.

Depending on the dilemma you face, it may be appropriate to bring key people into the process as you get started. It takes longer to decide in a group, but a variety of perspectives is more likely to yield the best outcome. Key stakeholders and influencers can speak positively and help you stay committed to a decision they helped make. Each step of Story Shaping can be completed in a team or as an individual.

In every dilemma, our first step should be to ask the Author of all stories for wisdom. It is always wise to pray for God's wisdom, and prayer should saturate the Story-Shaping process (James 1:5). Once we have earnestly sought God, it is time to read the backstory of the dilemma.

A. WHAT IS HAPPENING?

The core activity in reading the backstory, or what I will also call the "old story," since the aim of Story Shaping is writing better new stories, is identifying what is happening. In some cases, this can be done easily. You may be able to determine what is happening on your own. Writing a sentence or two about the current situation and what is healthy, unhealthy, and risky about it provides an objective description that you can test for its accuracy and use as a guidepost for gauging future progress. Writing may seem an unnecessary effort when you are facing a big challenge, but crises can seem overwhelming until we articulate them. Often, we are afraid to tackle the monster that looms so large. Once we figure out what the monster is, we may discover we have been running from a kitten.

If the dilemma you face affects an organization, it is best to gather a variety of perspectives. People have different ideas about what is happening and why. Be careful how you gather information. Too many times the information-gathering process can turn negative. Because there is a problem to solve, it is natural to focus on the problem, but such a focus can also be negative and doubt producing rather than inspiring and faith producing. David Cooperrider and Suresh Srivastva sought to change this negative aspect of information gathering by developing a process called Appreciative Inquiry (AI). AI first asks questions about the existing strengths of an organization and uses those to determine what must not be eliminated when change is made. These bright spots can serve as inspiration when decision makers get to step 3 in Story Shaping: Craft a New Story.[3]

As you gather data about what is happening, write down a concise description. Think carefully about the statement. Make sure it addresses what you see and understand to be the real issue. You can also clarify what you do not know at this point.

B. WHY IS IT HAPPENING?

When you are not feeling well and visit a doctor, she is likely to ask several questions and take your vital signs for a preliminary diagnosis. She may even order blood or urine tests to diagnose the cause of your problem. A sore throat and an upset stomach are symptoms, but various illnesses cause them. These illnesses are remedied by different treatments. What may cure one illness may exacerbate another. Getting a correct diagnosis is thus essential for achieving a cure.

Similarly, in Story Shaping, we want the best diagnosis possible when dealing with a challenging situation. As you begin, you may or may not understand all the factors at work in your situation, but it is helpful to identify what you know for sure, what you think could be factors, and what is unclear.

The nature of the dilemma you face will determine the factors you should examine most closely to answer the *why* question. Looking for repeated patterns in likely causes is a good place to start. If you have been fired from more than one job, what was common in each situation? Was it the type of work, your attitude, or is this career field not a good fit for you? Don't assume your problems are someone else's fault. If relationships have been a challenge, what have people said? Are there some habits or behaviors you can change before starting again? When dealing with a serious interpersonal or organizational conflict, it may be best to start by identifying the interpretive lenses of those involved. (See chapter 4 for a full explanation of these lenses and how they work.)

Briefly chart your own beliefs, ethics, values, and reasoning from the left lens (LL), plus any impulses from the right lens (RL) related to the dilemma. List your best guess about the lenses of the others involved and how they function in the situation. It may be appropriate to confirm with others that you are accurately describing their perspective. Ask what lenses are affecting your own thoughts, attitudes, and behaviors. Determine which of your beliefs, ethics, and values most affect your feelings about the issue. Another person who does not share your perspective may not feel the same way about the situation.

Determine what lenses are affecting others' thoughts, attitudes, and behaviors. Ask what matters most to them. Perhaps a conflict is due to divergent ethics or values. Understanding the differences between you and the others involved will maximize your efforts.

If you did an Appreciative Inquiry, be sure to reflect on that too. Remember, you do not just want to find out about problems in a situation. Identifying what is working well can also be useful. Healthy systems can aid in resolving a situation.

What other circumstances are at play? Many dilemmas are a result of the unexpected. An unforeseen job loss can create a great deal of stress in a marriage. If a tornado destroyed your home, you may be facing a major financial crisis. The loss of a sizable employer in a community can affect prospects for related small businesses. Identify the circumstances that are factors in your dilemma. It is also good to determine whether these factors are likely to continue.

Is the situation you are confronting a recurring problem or something new? This question clarifies the nature of your dilemma. Some issues are one-time challenges that just need a good one-time decision to resolve. Other issues, such as bad habits, ongoing relational division, and chronic ineffectiveness, require a more thorough approach. In the case of a chronic problem, identify the steps taken in the past to address it and seek to determine why they did not work. We often continue doing the same things to try to solve chronic issues to no avail. Albert Einstein is often misattributed with this cliché definition of insanity: "Doing the same thing over and over and expecting different results." Rightly ascribed or not, the message is clear. If you have tried something multiple times and it has not worked, it is not likely to work next time. Try another solution.

When others are involved, be sure to ask for their ideas on why previous attempts at resolution failed. We can become so wedded to our own habits and ideas that we fail to see their weaknesses. As a professor, I encourage students to have friends proofread their papers before submitting them. I regularly write emails with typographic errors simply because I do not notice that they do not say what I want them to say, even after a quick proofread. I see what I want my emails to say, not what they actually say. The fresh eyes of a friend who did not write the email are more likely to catch my mistakes.

As you read the backstory, the old story, and determine why what is happening is happening, you are likely to discover root causes to problems that will need to be addressed or eliminated for a positive resolution. Note these.

Remember, however, that when change is needed, it can be tempting to change everything: fire the whole staff, tear the house down, end the relationship. In most cases, there remain many good things in a difficult situation that can and should be preserved. Look for the bright spots. It is more difficult and expensive to build a house from the ground up than it is to repaint the walls. Whatever stands out that should be retained, note it as a part of your long-term plan.

C. WHAT SHOULD COME OUT OF THE STORY-SHAPING PROCESS?

By this time, you have a good understanding of the old story. You have identified what is happening and determined possible factors and the perspectives of those involved. You may have noticed some things that should be eliminated, some you can fix, and others you should keep. The next step is to identify what you want from the Story-Shaping process. You may need to make a single decision. Perhaps a conflict needs to be resolved or a plan developed or implemented. This is your opportunity to evaluate whether things are healthy or whether improvements are needed. Taking into account what you learned from reading the backstory, write a simple statement of exactly what you want to gain by reshaping this story.

Now it is time to seek the Author of all our stories for his help and guidance as you decide on a course of action and begin to write a new story.

CHAPTER SIX

STEP 2: CATCH GOD'S STORY

The goal of Story Shaping is to collaborate with God in shaping your story—and those of your friends, family, church, company, and other groups you're a part of—by making better decisions. Story Shaping integrates the principles of practical theology, which seeks to "interpret the revelatory realism of God's action in concrete, lived experience."[1] In other words, Story Shaping expects God to be at work in our everyday lives. The second major step, Catch God's Story, acknowledges that in some cases, God's work and desire for us is clear. In other cases, God's presence is more subtle, and his will takes effort to discover.

Theological reflection is a phrase used in practical theology to describe the process of seeking God's will for an individual or church in a particular situation. I use the phrase "Catch God's Story" to describe theological reflection in Story Shaping because, first, it recognizes God is already at work. The title of Leonard Sweet's book, *Nudge: Awakening Each Other to the God Who's Already There*,[2] captures this idea powerfully. He writes that we can help others come to know the God who is already at work in their lives by leading them to faith in Christ. God is at work in our own lives too, and we can nudge ourselves to recognize what God may be doing and saying as we consider important decisions.

The second concept the phrase Catch God's Story captures is that effort is required. If you decide to join a softball league and play in the outfield, you are not likely to catch many fly balls unless you are willing to keep an eye on the batter, run to where the ball is likely to land, and carefully track the ball into your mitt. Catching fly balls takes effort. Catching God's story does too.

The third concept embedded in the phrase Catch God's Story is that it is God's story we want to catch. Other people want things from us. We have our own motives too, some of them selfish. But the goal for Christ-followers is to follow Christ, to live out his story. He is the real Author of our stories, so he should be our authority. We need to seek out God's story intentionally.

The fourth and final concept is that catching God's story is voluntary, not forced. Just as we can choose to read a novel or not, we can seek and adopt God's story or reject it.[3] We can choose to embrace and live out his story, receiving the benefit that comes from a vital relationship with God, or ignore his story or pretend it does not exist and suffer the consequences of that decision.

A study of the Old and New Testaments shows us that, at times, God intervenes miraculously in human situations. We see it in the parting of the Red Sea for Moses and the Israelites (Exodus 14) and in Jesus's birth to the Virgin Mary (Luke 1 and 2). But Scripture is also clear about human responsibility for our decisions and actions. Joshua told the newly settled Israelites to "choose for yourselves this day whom you will serve" (Joshua 24:15). Every command in the Bible implies that people, by God's grace, have the responsibility to carry out what has been commanded. Whether or not God intervenes in our situations, we each have the responsibility to do the right thing. Our decisions make a difference, and, in many cases, our decisions may cause us to obey God or disobey God.

If you are a committed Christian, obeying Jesus should be

your first priority in every decision. The Bible speaks clearly to many issues we will face. Should I be faithful to my spouse? Yes, absolutely. Should I rob a store? No. The Ten Commandments forbid robbery and adultery, and Christ and the apostles in the New Testament reaffirm these commands. But the Bible does not explicitly address many other questions we face in today's world. What chapter and verse could you read to decide whether you should buy an iPhone or an Android? We need a way to apply God's clear direction to our own particular situations in all times and places.

Catching God's story means finding out what God wants us to do in the decisions we face. It involves pursuing wisdom from the three sources to which Christians have always turned: the Bible, the Holy Spirit, and the Christian community.[4]

A. LOOK FOR APPLICABLE BIBLICAL COMMANDS AND EXAMPLES

Christians turn to the Scriptures as their first step for guidance. They believe the Bible is "not just a book about what God has done in the past but is first and foremost about God's direct and immediate word for their lives in the present."[5] Christians affirm the Bible is God inspired and uniquely trustworthy and authoritative. It provides the truth about God and humankind. The collection of books that make up the biblical canon, often called the Holy Bible, was established after an extensive process by the fourth-century church, in which every book was carefully evaluated for its reliability and authority. Nearly all branches of the Christian church have accepted that canon as their final authority.

Yet readers must interpret Scripture. The words of the Bible were written long ago, and it takes thought to determine how to apply them in our situations. It can be easy to twist the meaning of words, and different churches and theologians may interpret certain texts and their implications differently. However, we do not need to be paralyzed in seeking guidance from the Scriptures.

Mark Strauss writes, "The Holy Spirit living in the believer is the same Spirit who inspired the authors of Scripture so that, essentially, when we are reading Scripture, the Spirit is explaining the Spirit."[6] Amos Yong encourages us to allow the Holy Spirit to speak through the Scriptures alongside the Christian community of all ages, bearing witness and passing judgment (1 Corinthians 14:29) and helping us interpret and apply God's message to our churches and lives.[7] The Christian community, past and present, guards against inaccurate interpretations. "The community must discern what the text means and how that meaning is lived out . . . . Not all interpretations are equally valid; some are simply wrong. The interpretive community will decide which are and are not acceptable."[8]

Responsible biblical interpretation is essential to discern whether a command or action described in the Bible still applies today. One example of the need for discernment can be found in the dietary laws listed in Leviticus 11. God forbade the Hebrews to eat many specific animals. This would seem to be a clear biblical prohibition. But in Acts 10, the apostle Peter was on the roof of Simon the tanner's house when he had a vision of a sheet descending that included all those previously forbidden animals. A voice said, "Get up, Peter. Kill and eat." Peter protested that he had never eaten any unclean food, but the voice spoke again, "Do not call anything impure that God has made clean." This happened three times (vv. 13–16). Most Christians throughout history have interpreted this passage as God granting Christians the freedom to eat foods previously forbidden.

Another example is the replacement of the Old Testament sacrificial system by Jesus Christ's sacrifice on the cross. This replacement echoes throughout the New Testament, but especially in Hebrews 9:11–12: "When Christ came as high priest of the good things that are now already here, . . . he entered the Most Holy Place once for all by his own blood, thus obtaining eternal redemption." When we read Old Testament commands to offer animal sacrifices to God as acts of worship, we understand that Christ fulfilled and replaced those sacrifices by sacrificing himself on our behalf on the cross. You do not need to bring a live lamb to church next Sunday for a sacrifice.

CLEAR COMMANDS	IMPLIED PRINCIPLES	CLEAR PROHIBITIONS
• Repeated in the New Testament	• Examples & situations similar to yours	• Repeated in the New Testament
• Never opposed elsewhere in Scripture	• Instructions relevant today	• Never countered elsewhere in scriptire
• Applying to all	• Relevant OT instruction	• Applying to all

NOT ADDRESSED
• No biblical reference or examples
• Issues not relevant in biblical times

We must be careful as we seek to determine which biblical commands and examples are relevant to our situation, but the Bible has much to say to help us decide. Clear New Testament commands are a good starting place. We know Jesus's Golden Rule: "Do to others what you would have them do to you" (Matthew 7:12). If one of my options involves taking advantage of another person or causing them pain I would not choose for myself, it is clear this is not something I should do. Many other instructions in the Bible apply in all places and all times too, even if we are not always eager to put them into practice. As Mark Twain is supposed to have said, "It ain't those parts of the Bible that I can't understand that bother me, it is the parts that I do understand." If a decision you are facing relates to clear New Testament instructions, follow them.

When issues we face do not relate to clear, specific commands, we can often find guidance from the examples of biblical characters. Much of the Bible is narrative. It reads as an account of what happened as people lived their lives and experienced God's work in, through, and around them. We can distill life principles from these narrative passages.[9] For example, Genesis 50:15–21 says that after Jacob died, eleven of his sons were afraid that their brother Joseph, whom they had sold into slavery, might seek to take revenge on them. He certainly had a right to get even. Joseph's brothers feared he had only been kind to them because their beloved father was alive, with the goal of settling accounts after Jacob passed away. But Joseph responded to their fears with these unforgettable words, "You intended to harm me, but God intended it for good" (v. 20). Joseph's words and actions provide a wonderful example of forgiveness and reconciliation that we can and should still implement today. This is only one of thousands of life principles we can discover in the Bible and apply directly to decisions we face.

Many people throughout history have interpreted the Bible allegorically to apply it to their situations. Although there have been instances in which people have taken passages of the Bible, applied them in ways other than they were originally meant, and seen good things happen, there have also been horrible failures. We can make the Bible say almost anything we want if we seek an application beyond the meaning of the text itself. For example, someone might use Jesus's parable of the treasure hidden in the field in Matthew 13:44 to conclude God wants him to invest in a metal detector business. While the business may be profitable, this interpretation of the Bible is not. The point of Jesus's parable was that the kingdom of heaven is more valuable than anything else.

To be ready to apply Bible passages to our situations, we need to know the Bible well and know how to interpret it accurately. Regular personal Bible study and learning from good biblical preaching, teaching, and writing can help us grow in these regards. Gordon Fee and Douglas Stuart's classic book on biblical interpretation, *How to Read the Bible for All Its Worth*, is excellent for learning how to interpret and apply the Bible. Studying the Scriptures is a lifelong process best done in cooperation with others in the body of Christ.

B. LISTEN TO THE HOLY SPIRIT

Before leaving his disciples, Jesus promised them it was to their advantage that he would go away, because in his place he would send the Holy Spirit who would lead them into all truth (John 14:16; 16:7, 13). The New Testament gives several examples of the Holy Spirit providing direction to the apostles through dreams, visions, prophecy, and being "led by the Spirit." Christian jargon often calls this last form of guidance "the still small voice," drawing from Elijah's experience in 1 Kings 19:11–14 when God did not speak through an earthquake, fire, or a mighty rock-crushing wind. Instead, God's voice came in a "gentle whisper," translated as a "still small voice" in the King James Version. The Bible does not detail exactly what Holy Spirit guidance is, but the common experiences of Spirit-filled believers through the centuries seems to square with Elijah's account.

Many believers around the world have reported receiving what they would call divine guidance.[10] Longtime professor of philosophy at the University of Southern California Dallas Willard advocates in *Hearing God* for an "ongoing conversation with God" in which hearing from him is part of the believer's regular experience.[11] An email poll of attenders of Willow Creek

Community Church near Chicago tallied more than five hundred replies from those who had experienced divine whispers.[12] Mark Batterson calls supernatural ideas that come seemingly out of nowhere "God ideas." He says, "I'd rather have one God idea than a thousand good ideas. Good ideas are good, but God ideas change the world."[13]

A study of divine guidance in the New Testament seems to indicate four levels of clarity and certainty in messages from God. The highest level is miraculous and obvious to more than one person. On the Day of Pentecost, thousands of people heard the sound of a rushing wind and saw tongues of fire rest on the Christian disciples, then heard them speak in other languages. This experience affirmed Peter's words and led to about three thousand accepting his invitation to repent and be baptized for the forgiveness of their sins (see Acts 2). The voice of God speaking to confirm Jesus's ministry at his baptism (Matthew 3:17, Mark 1:11, and Luke 3:22), at his transfiguration (Matthew 17:5, Mark 9:7, and Luke 9:35), and in John 12:28 was heard by many people. All these witnesses could have given legal testimony about the messages they heard. In Acts 9, Jesus dramatically and unmistakably spoke to Paul. He was traveling to Damascus with some men when Jesus appeared as a bright light, blinded him, and spoke to him audibly. There was no mistaking it as a hallucination. Even the other men heard the voice and could tell he was blinded (see Acts 9:3–7).

The second-highest level of divine guidance occurs when an individual receives a clear message from God with another believer confirming its authenticity. In 1 Corinthians 14:29–32 Paul tells the church to allow prophets to bear witness to the prophetic messages received by others. The Greek word used in the passage is related to judgment and could imply rational discernment rather than a supernatural ability to confirm the divine source of a message. But a Holy Spirit–given ability to tell whether a message is from God is likely what Paul meant, since 1 Corinthians 12:10 lists the noun form of the same Greek word to describe the spiritual gift of "distinguishing between spirits." As we saw in chapter 3, Acts 13 records a season of corporate worship and fasting in Antioch during which "the Holy Spirit said, 'Set apart for me Barnabas and Saul'" (v. 2). Although the passage's wording does not describe exactly how it happened, the implication is that the Spirit spoke through one of the prophets present, with others confirming the message's authenticity.

Wilfredo "Choco" De Jesus pastors New Life Covenant Church in Chicago. Under his leadership, the church has grown to become one of the most influential churches in the country, launching many ministries that assist all kinds of people in Chicagoland. *Time* magazine recognized him as one of the 100 Most Influential People in the World in 2013, but, at age fourteen, he was just a poor kid in a single-parent home in one of Chicago's roughest neighborhoods. A group of teens invited him to a special church service. He went and gave his life to Jesus. An older woman came to pray with him and said, "God has a message for you: 'I have called you to be a great leader. Stay in my path. I will bless those who bless you, and I will curse those who curse you.'" Choco had rarely been to church, let alone heard a prophecy before, but twenty minutes later, while boarding an elevator to leave the meeting, a man stepped in and said, "Have you not heard? I've called to you to be a great leader. Stay in my path. I will bless those who bless you, and I will curse those who curse you."[14] We can now see that God fulfilled that promise, which was incredibly confirmed by two people in nearly the same words on the same day.

Dennis Lum has compiled the results of a variety of empirical studies on prophecy, including his own study, to determine common ways people receive prophetic messages. They can come in single words, phrases, complete sentences, visual images, or general impressions.[15] Dramatic, uncontrollable, ecstatic behavior is rare for those who receive prophecies. Though a strong sense of urgency to share the message often accompanies it, that sense of urgency is relieved when the person shares the message with others. Lum found in his study that most messages were comforting and encouraging, which can provide confirmation to those who may be sensing God's leading.[16] Lum counsels, "The faith community must be instructed to judge all prophetic proclamations against the established teachings of the Bible and to exercise spiritual discernment."[17]

The third level of divine guidance is an individual's clear sense of a message from God without confirmation from others. While in Ephesus, Paul felt a prompting to take an offering to Jerusalem even though it risked his imprisonment. Prophetic words warned him and those traveling with him that bonds awaited. His friends begged him not to go, but in Acts 21:13–14, Paul answered, "Why are you weeping and breaking my heart? I am ready not only to be bound, but also to die in Jerusalem for the name of the Lord Jesus." His friends then replied, "The Lord's will be done." It was apparently the still, small voice of God's conviction, which only Paul heard, that drove him on. In Acts 20:22 he described this sense of divine guidance for the mission as being "compelled by the Spirit." In instances of this third level of guidance, Christians often say they received a clear sense of what needed to be done or an awareness of information they could not have obtained naturally. Some talk about a feeling of burning or a "burden," a term related to a Hebrew word that can also be translated "load" and is used in the Old Testament to describe several prophets' divinely imparted messages. The word can literally mean a heavy load to carry.[18]

My own conversion involved a clear and unmistakable message from God that no one else heard, and I have personally experienced spiritual guidance at this level on many occasions. Sometimes these divine personal messages are verbal. As the Christian rock band Newsboys said many years ago, "Sometimes it works a bit like a teleprompter."[19] Although some Christian leaders question the Spirit's active guidance in the world today, the Bible affirms the Spirit's ministry will continue until Jesus's return.

The fourth and lowest level of divine guidance is the most subtle and may not be present in the New Testament. Some Christians describe it as a presence or lack of peace. The most common Greek word for peace is not used in this manner in the New Testament, but many examples of guidance by the Holy Spirit could have come about in this way.[20] In 2 Corinthians 2:12–13, the apostle Paul describes having an open door of opportunity for ministry in Troas but "no peace of mind," so he moved on to Macedonia.[21] Believers today often report a transcendent lack of emotional well-being that is different from natural fear when faced with decisions. They may perceive this "lack of peace" as evidence of God directing them another way.

Seeking God's voice brings challenges, though. What may seem like divine guidance could actually come from another source. For example, our own emotions speak loudly to us. Without clear discernment, we may convince ourselves that what we want is what God wants. There are far too many stories of well-meaning Christian young men approaching attractive Christian women, saying, "God wants us to get married." Afraid of the consequences of fighting God, some women have agreed without further confirmation and found themselves in painfully unpleasant marriages wondering, "Was this God's will or a man who could not tell the difference between his hormones and the Holy Spirit?"

We also know that Satan deceives people whenever possible (John 13:2; 2 Corinthians 2:11; Revelation 12:9). There is a risk that what seems like God's voice may not be. When I served as a pastor, people often visited me with claims of hearing God tell them to do crazy things. In one week, two people came to my office claiming to be John the Baptist, come to prepare the way for the return of the Lord Jesus. They could not both have been right, and Jesus has not returned yet. I have even seen people committed to mental health facilities after uttering "prophetic" words in God's name that had no basis whatsoever.

Certainly one of the risks of being open to divine revelation is getting it wrong. As Andrew Root writes, "It is possible that our experiences of God are truly that, but it is also possible that we are confused or misguided."[22] This has led some to suppress seeking or heeding extrabiblical divine revelation. Some do so for theological reasons. Others simply do not think it worth the risk. The fastest-growing segment of the church during the past hundred years is the Pentecostal, charismatic, and renewalist movement. Central to their beliefs is a conviction that God still speaks through his Holy Spirit. Yet prophecy, words of knowledge, and speaking in tongues with interpretation, which used to characterize nearly all Pentecostal and charismatic worship services, are now rare in many of these churches. If God does want to speak through his Spirit, we miss a lot if we do not listen and follow what he says.

This brings us to Paul's closing instruction in his first letter to the Thessalonians. "Do not quench the Spirit. Do not treat prophecies with contempt but test them all; hold on to what is good" (1 Thessalonians 5:19–21). Note that we can quench the Spirit's work. The Greek word literally means to put out a fire. God will not force himself on us. If we do not seek the Spirit's direction, he will not speak. That is why verse 20 tells us not to despise prophecies. We should not dismiss something out of hand because it is unusual or uncomfortable. But even though God can and does often speak through his Spirit, we can also get it wrong.

We should test everything and adhere only to that which is good. So how can we test extrabiblical revelations?

God can sometimes use prophetic words from others to confirm his internal direction to us. I lived and ministered in the state of Washington for eighteen years. The last five of those I taught full time at Northwest University near Seattle and served part time at a large multi-site church. It was a wonderful season of life and ministry. I loved my students and the churches I got to work with. I had no plans to leave, when I got an unexpected phone call from Dr. Bill Hackett, provost of Southeastern University in Lakeland, Florida, inviting me to serve as the dean for Southeastern's College of Christian Ministries and Religion. I was shocked. Florida was not on my "dream sheet," as we used to call our Air Force assignment request forms. I had no desire to leave Washington, but I wanted to be open to what God would have me do.

I came home that night and shared the opportunity with my wife and children. They were far more encouraging than I expected. We prayed, then accepted the offer to fly out and see the campus. I shared the opportunity with my dean and president at Northwest, and both reluctantly (not wanting to lose me) encouraged me that I would do well in the role. My doctoral mentor, the renowned author Leonard Sweet, had recently spoken at Southeastern and urged me to consider the position.

The most amazing confirmation occurred two weeks later when I flew back to Florida for interviews with the administration and faculty. After only a couple of hours of sleep on a red-eye flight and more than twelve hours of interviews, I remembered a personal message I had received on Facebook exactly a week before the first call from Southeastern. The message was from Jennifer Lorentzen, a member of the church I used to pastor. I had not seen her in almost three years, but here is what she'd written:

Hi Pastor Alan! You have been on my mind lately. When I prayed and asked the Lord why you are on my mind and your name has been coming out of my mouth, He showed me transparent flames of fire. I am sure this is a very good thing. I know that fire that burns very hot is transparent like jet fuel. I feel like the Lord is doing something amazing or about to do something amazing in your life, and ministry. Does this mean anything to you?

When I received this message, I had no idea what was about to happen, so I wrote back, "Wow, thanks, Jennifer. I am not sure what it means. I really enjoy teaching at Northwest, but I am always up for whatever God has." She replied with another message detailing the image of me in the midst of fire and sending out flames all over the globe.

I remembered that message a month later while sitting at dinner with some of Southeastern University's leadership team. I shared the story with one of the vice presidents and showed him the message on my phone. He laughed, then pointed to the logo on his polo shirt. I noticed afresh the image of Southeastern University's mascot, prominently displayed—fire.

Of course, fire is a biblical image for the Holy Spirit, and an appropriate mascot for a Pentecostal school, but the Holy Spirit used that otherwise inexplicable circumstance to confirm his desire for us to move across the country. I am grateful he did. This story is one of many in my life in which what seemed to be God's direction was confirmed by others and by the ultimate outcome.

I have talked to thousands who also have experienced what they firmly believe was supernatural guidance. Several excellent books include stories of divine direction and principles on seeking and discerning God's voice in one's life.

Leonard Sweet and Frank Viola's *Jesus Speaks* shares tips

on hearing from God drawn from a narrative retelling of Jesus's encounters with his followers after the cross and before his ascension. "Jesus is always speaking to his followers," they write. "It is up to us to learn how to recognize his voice."[23] Although they rightfully advocate seeking to hear Jesus's voice through Scripture first and using it to test anything else we may think we hear from him, they also encourage Christians to continually seek the voice of the Lord, who is always speaking, sometimes through our thoughts, emotions, and desires. They say Jesus also speaks through wisdom, visions, dreams, audible voices, our conscience, and other Christians.[24]

Sweet and Viola suggest asking God for direction when it is needed, putting yourself in a posture in which God can speak to you, perhaps walking, worshiping, or in morning devotions. Fasting may help attune our spiritual ears to the Lord's voice.[25]

Sweet and Viola propose four ways to tell the difference between the Lord's voice and our own thoughts:

1. The Lord's voice will always be in harmony with Scripture and love for others.
2. The disposition will never be one of hastiness, anger, jealousy, arrogance, or anxiety.
3. Confidence will come from an inward knowing that the word is from the Holy Spirit and not one's own mind.
4. The impressions left on us will be life, peace, insight, and unwavering duration.[26]

If you seek the Lord's direction but have not heard from him after a sustained period, they suggest "you (may) already know the answer deep in your heart."[27]

Loren Cunningham is founder of one of the world's largest missions organizations, Youth with a Mission (YWAM).

In *Is That Really You, God?* he recounts how he was led to start YWAM on the principle that God speaks, and nothing should be done until he directs. Sometimes this principle has meant the YWAM leadership team seeks God's direction for an entire night. YWAM's main base and its University of the Nations is in Kona, Hawaii, because of guidance received at 5:30 a.m. during such a prayer vigil.[28] Cunningham's principles for hearing God include:

- Submit to Jesus's lordship and be willing to do whatever he asks.
- Resist the enemy.
- Expect an answer.
- Allow God to speak in the way he chooses.
- Confess unforgiven sin.
- Be sure you have obeyed the last thing God asked you to do.
- Get your own leading.
- Don't talk about your guidance until God gives you permission.
- Get confirmation from other spiritually sensitive people.
- Beware of counterfeits.
- Remember, sometimes the opposition of man is guidance from God.
- Recognizing God's voice gets easier with practice.
- Relationship with God is the most important reason to hear him.[29]

Dallas Willard provides a thorough theology of God's voice in *Hearing God*. Willard acknowledges God speaks in a variety of ways, including the Bible, dreams, visions, angelic visitations, voices, and extraordinary events. Yet he says "the 'still small voice'—or the 'interior' voice, as it is sometimes called—is the primary form (preferred by God), in which God individually addresses those who walk with him in a mature, conversational relationship, proclaiming and showing forth the Kingdom of God."[30] Willard refers to "Three Lights" that Christians have historically used to discern God's voice:

1. The Scriptures
2. Inner impulses from the Holy Spirit
3. Circumstances[31]

He acknowledges that this three-pronged approach can cause difficulties, "yet, all who have much experience in The Way of Christ will know that it is *somehow* right to look for guidance in circumstances, the Bible, and inner impulses. And all will know that these three *somehow* serve to correct each other."[32]

Here are some "filters" to test what might be a divine whisper:

- Is the prompting truly from God? Take time to ask God.
- Is it scriptural? Messages that contradict the Bible are not from God.
- Is it wise? God's whispers rarely go against common sense.
- Is it in tune with your own character? God's whispers are usually affirmed from several sources in a variety of ways.
- What do the people you most trust think about it? Ask the wisdom of those further down the spiritual path.[33]
- Is it specific and something you would not normally know or consider?[34]
- Does the sense of direction or guidance and the urgency to fulfill it stay strong or decrease over time?[35]

All the writers surveyed in this section acknowledge that hearing God's voice is a skill developed over a lifetime. We are fallible people serving an infallible God. This is likely why one of the nine gifts of the Holy Spirit identified in 1 Corinthians 12 is distinguishing between spirits. God places some people in the Christian community who have a supernatural gift to determine whether a message or impression is truly from God. So earnestly seek the Holy Spirit's wisdom and direction, but test everything, usually with the help of your Christian family (see James 1:5–6; 1 Corinthians 12:31; Proverbs 3:5–7, 13–20). Something that comes to you internally yet seems beyond you and would not normally cross your mind warrants consideration as a possible message from the Spirit. Thoughts from him usually do not pass quickly but recur, often with a sense of urgency. Look for confirmation from others and circumstances, but especially from the Holy Spirit himself.

C. SEEK WISDOM AND CONFIRMATION FROM THE CHRISTIAN COMMUNITY

When Scripture does not speak directly to a dilemma and you do not receive clear direction from the Holy Spirit, the Christian community can play a role in discerning what God may desire for the situation. We saw earlier that James, as leader of the early church, summarized the final decision of the Jerusalem Council with the words, "It seemed good to the Holy Spirit and to us" (Acts 15:28). God's confirmation of the best decision came as his people worked together to seek his will. As Bryan Koch and Daniel McNaughton highlight in their excellent manual for spiritual growth, *Follow*, God often speaks through his people, the church.[36]

There is a growing awareness in practical theology of the role the larger Christian community plays. The phrase "Christian community" can reflect a local congregation, but it usually encompasses the entire church of all generations, acknowledging the role of tradition, the studies of scholars through the years and around the world, as well as those familiar with the details of a particular congregation.[37]

There are many ways the Christian community can help us discern God's will in a dilemma. As mentioned in the previous section, one of these is confirming divine revelation. Sometimes the help of the Christian community can be natural rather than supernatural. Our leaders and friends can point out what we might miss on our own. If I get a piece of food in my teeth or something on my cheek, I will miss it unless I look in a mirror. But my wife will be quick to point it out, because she has an objective view. Friends and others can often see what we cannot. Sometimes our emotions and fears blind us to opportunities or to destructive habits. Someone near you may sense God is at work in you before you do. There is wisdom in the church, especially when we seek it from those we know to be wise and knowledgeable about us and the dilemmas we face. King Rehoboam would have been much better off listening to his father's older, wiser advisers. Instead, he listened to his friends, who may have known him but did not know how to run a kingdom (1 Kings 12:1–24).

As we saw in chapter 3, God still provides divine direction, but he does not always use supernatural guidance. What does that mean for us? It means we should be open to God's direction. We should pray and listen for God's voice, but we should not freeze in its absence.[38] James says to ask God for wisdom (James 1:5). Wisdom is the ability to make moral and practical decisions apart from specific, supernatural direction.[39] During the next step of Story Shaping, we will see how to employ whatever wisdom or guidance from the Holy Spirit we have received in crafting a new story.

CHAPTER SEVEN

STEP 3: CRAFT A NEW STORY

If you have walked through the first two steps of the Story-Shaping process, you will arrive at step 3 in one of three places:

1. You have a clear sense of God's direction in a decision, perhaps from the Bible or from the confirmed direction of the Holy Spirit. In this place, you will want to press on to the last section of this chapter, "Develop a Plan to Enact the Decision."

2. You may have an uncertain inclination about what you believe God is saying to you. In this place, I encourage you to walk through the following pages to "test" this leading and gain further wisdom.

3. Finally, you may have no sense of divine guidance in your decision. Do not be alarmed. As we saw earlier, even the apostle Paul did not receive divine revelation for most of his decisions. In this place, you will definitely want to follow step 3 carefully as you seek to make a good decision.

I use the phrase "Craft a New Story" to describe this step for several reasons:

1. The word *craft* denotes a willful yet creative decision about what you will do in your dilemma. *Craft* also implies you are not creating something out of nothing but are working with what you already have to produce a new and better outcome. Things will be different because of your decision.

2. It is *a* story rather than *the* story because, in all likelihood, you have many options from which to choose. It may be that more than one would be a good choice. Making major decisions can paralyze us if we assume one decision is perfect and all others are bad. How many people have continued as unwilling singles because they turned down proposals from well-meaning potential spouses they were not sure were their perfect soul mates? Mark Batterson writes that, as much as we love clear decisions with 90 percent or better certainty, most of our key choices are of the 52/48 variety, and we cannot always tell immediately which option is on the 52 percent side.[1] You may or may not end this step with one clear best decision, but, in all likelihood, *a* decision is much better than *no* decision.

3. I call this a *new* story because your decision will change the future for you and perhaps others. This is true even if, in some cases, the new story differs only slightly from the old.

You can use different tools to craft your story. When you are making repairs inside your house, you are not likely to use every tool in your toolbox. Similarly, when making a decision, you will rarely use every tool listed in this chapter. Yet a smart artisan appreciates a well-stocked toolbox and has the skills to use the tools it contains. In this section, I will show you several "tools"—techniques you can use in determining and evaluating the options—to help you craft your new story.

The first question to ask, when deciding which tools to use, is whether an individual or group decision would be best. If you are the only person the decision affects and the risk is low, deciding on your own is fine. But the stakes get higher the more people the decision impacts, the greater the uncertainty, the lower your expertise, and the higher the cost of a bad decision. In such a case, you may need to consider recruiting a decision-making team. Not every decision warrants getting others involved. Here are guidelines to determine whether a team decision is likely to be superior to an individual decision.

Individual decisions are usually best when:

- One of the following is true:
  - You are likely to be the only person significantly impacted.
  - Others involved are not willing to meet with you.
  - Others involved have not been good team members in the past or do not have sufficient perspective and emotional distance to decide objectively.
- You have the resources and knowledge needed to make a good decision.
- You need to decide quickly.

On the other hand, group decisions are usually best when:

- The decision will impact many people.
- Those affected hold several different viewpoints.
- Opposition to a final decision is likely, so having a representative from opposing groups on a decision team may alleviate some resistance.
- You do not have all the information or expertise needed to make a good decision.

- The decision will have a large impact on a group's future.
- The problem or issue is a chronic one with no clear solution.
- Conflict already exists among people, but they are willing to work together to find a solution.
- Enacting the plan will require many individuals.

If working with a team is the best way to craft a new story, choosing the right people is critical. Jim Collins found "getting the right people on the bus" was one of the first steps taken by corporations that made a leap from good to great. These companies did not hire positions. They hired people and found that the character and gifts of the individuals made more of an impact than having slots filled.[2] Many churches and businesses have adopted a Three C criteria that reflects this idea, hiring staff who not only have *competency* at the skills the job requires but also *character* and *chemistry*.[3] An individual's integrity and ability to work with others on the team is essential for the team's success.

In selecting the best story-crafting team possible, look for the following:

- People of character.
- People who work well with others.
- People who sincerely care about the future of the person, group, or organization.
- People representing the major groups or types of people affected.
- People with "adjustable lenses" who are willing to consider new possibilities and other ways of thinking.
- People who will speak their minds and risk disagreement.

We may not enjoy conflict, but one purpose of a group is to gather as many ideas as possible and wrestle through options. There must be a variety of opinions and ideas for this to occur, with an open culture that allows team members to express them. The facilitator of the group must establish up front that it is not a place for "yes people."

I served as lead pastor of a church that balanced power between the pastor and the governing board. Thus, I was never without at least two or three board members willing to challenge my ideas. I have had many pastor friends who resented such board members, but I discovered these vocal members loved Jesus, loved our church, and loved me. They simply wanted to make sure we made the best decisions possible. I learned to value their opposition. I did not always surrender my vision to their concerns, but there were times their wisdom highlighted issues I had neglected to notice. Listening to them prevented almost certain disaster. The best decision-making teams are willing to disagree, but do so in a constructive way that seeks the best of all involved. In *Creativity, Inc.*, Ed Catmull, one of the founders of Pixar, talks about how candor—the priority of providing honest feedback—was one of the most essential elements in Pixar obtaining excellence in both the technical and story aspects of its award-winning motion pictures.[4]

Another important consideration with groups is the number of people involved. The nature of a dilemma should drive the size of the team. Conflict resolution need involve only those in conflict and, possibly, a mediator. A personal decision may require only family members and a friend or two. An organizational decision will likely require three to twelve individuals. Remember, the more people on a team, the more time it will take to reach a decision and the more difficult it will be to gain consensus, but larger teams also generate more ideas and perspectives.

In the 1800s, gold rushes took place all over the North American West. The California Gold Rush of 1849 may be the most famous, but Nevada, Colorado, the Yukon, and many other places experienced their own rush of "prospectors" hoping to find a gold or silver vein and become rich.

The prospectors got their nickname because they did not know exactly where they would find gold. But they did have a basic idea of what to look for. They knew gold veins typically yielded small samples into streams, so the prospector's favorite tools were the gold pan (to see which streams yielded gold dust) and the pick (to find the vein after they found an ore-bearing stream). Once a prospector found a promising mountainside, he could not tell how large a vein might be or how pure the ore was until much mining had taken place. One thing was certain. If a prospector did not prospect, he would find nothing.

I call the main decision-making component of Crafting a New Story prospecting because of the uncertain nature of most solutions. Decision scientists Chip and Dan Heath have found that businesses and individuals often fail to make the best decisions because of "narrow framing."[5] This term refers to an assumption that there will be a clear right decision or a simple choice between two options, what the Heaths call "Either/Or Thinking."

Whether you work with a team or go it alone, there are usually many possible good decisions to make. This is why step 3 of Story Shaping is called Crafting *a* New Story rather than Writing *the* New Story. Some options may be better than others, but it will not usually be possible to know the best one until after the decision point. Like a good prospector, you can employ some tricks to finding good ore-bearing streams to lead you to the mother lode. The goal is simple: generate as many solutions as possible, narrow them to a manageable list, evaluate each option, and then make the best decision possible.

A. INCREASE THE NUMBER OF OPTIONS

Many times when faced with a decision, we see only one or two options. We may miss the best decision because we cannot see more possibilities. Chapter 4 described the lenses we all use to understand the world. Our belief layer is usually limited. We believe we understand more than we actually do about the options in front of us. We forget we are wearing any lenses at all. Yet it is critical to expand our options if we are to find the best possibilities.

As alluded to earlier, most choices are not either/or opportunities. Viewing a choice in this way limits our possibility thinking. Brain researchers John Kounlos and Mark Beeman have conducted a number of studies to determine what happens when people experience an "Aha!" moment of insight. They write, "Everything you do has the potential to limit what you do next. Everything you think has the potential to limit what you think next. And you won't even know this is happening. . . . Your past informs your assumptions, beliefs, expectations but also limits your ability to think and act flexibly."[6]

Good Story Shaping fights the limits of either/or thinking by seeking as many creative options as possible. If you are facing a personal decision, pull out a notepad or your computer and write down every idea that comes to mind. Don't limit yourself at this point. Don't get stuck in the "either this or that" mindset. There is always another option.

In 1953 Alex Faickney Osborne popularized the concept of brainstorming in his book *Applied Imagination*. The process has been widely used in group creativity and problem-solving situations. Usually the process involves a facilitator clarifying an objective, with members of the team then speaking as many ideas as they can imagine with no limits related to viability or absurdity.[7]

When well facilitated in a group that feels free to share and be creative, brainstorming can lead to creative solutions. The keys are:

1. Let the ideas flow.
2. Write them down.
3. Suppress comments and attitudes that stifle creativity (for example, "That is stupid. That won't work.").
4. Encourage people to dream without boundaries as ideas are shared.

In my own experience leading brainstorming groups on many occasions, the ideas that seemed the craziest, while not adopted themselves, often enabled people to begin to think in new ways and led to the options the groups ultimately adopted.

However, studies have also shown that many times brainstorming actually reduces the number of options generated. Individuals in such studies came up with more ideas on their own than in groups. Several factors can stifle group creativity. One is blocking. This is when a person has an idea to share but another takes the floor first. While that first idea is being recorded, the individual who has not yet shared forgets the other idea.[8] Another is fixation. This is the tendency for others' ideas to influence people to the extent that they stop sharing their own.[9]

Decision-making teams can overcome the limiting factors of brainstorming by practicing a combination of private and public brainstorming. I usually ask brainstorming team members to write a list of their own ideas privately first and then give them to the facilitator, who compiles everyone's ideas in front of the whole team to "prime the pump" and get more ideas flowing. A good facilitator will make sure all voices have a chance to speak, maximizing the flow of original thinking before blocking or fixation happens.

Other innovations can also harvest the benefits of cooperative group decision-making, while eliminating blocking and dominance by more vocal members. Some have used networked computers to share ideas in real time. This approach evens the field for less verbal participants.[10] Another approach is called 6–3–5 Brain-Writing. It involves six individuals meeting in a room together. A facilitator shares the rules, including forbidding any speaking during the sessions, and describes the dilemma the group will seek to resolve. Individuals receive a piece of paper with the dilemma stated at the top. Each member then has five minutes to write down three ideas. Group members write down any ideas they have, even crazy ones. At the end of five minutes, individuals pass their papers to the right. After looking over items on the list of the person to their left, they then write down new ideas or add to those already presented. Each member's goal is to write down three new or modified ideas in five minutes. The process continues until all members have written on all pages. The facilitator gathers the 108 ideas on all the sheets and either individually selects a final decision or processes the ideas with the participants to seek a consensus for a group decision.[11]

Another tool to help generate ideas is expanding questions. Because we tend to get stuck in certain lenses, we need to be encouraged to view things in a new way. Here are some examples of expanding questions:

> What would you do if you were guaranteed to succeed and had unlimited resources?
> What would _____ (Jesus, the apostle Paul, Albert Einstein, Yoda, Ronald Reagan, my successor, my predecessor, my best friend) do?
> What would you do if you could not do any of the options selected so far?
> What are we giving up by making this choice?
> Envision the best future possible. What did we do to get there?

In his book on creative thinking called *Smartcuts*, Shane Snow tells the story of his college roommate who set the world record for the video game *Super Mario Bros*. He did not win by beating every boss on every level, as most people sought to do in the game. Instead, he discovered secret "warp pipes" hidden in the game by the developers that enabled those who took them to pass through multiple levels without a single obstacle. Snow uses those pipes as a metaphor for what he calls "smartcuts"—ways to skip the normal steps others must take to gain success quickly. He provides examples from a variety of fields to show that a step-by-step process is not always or even usually the best process to follow.[12]

Snow advocates instead for "Lateral Thinking," a concept he borrowed from a living legend of creative thought, Edward De Bono. De Bono encourages putting on a variety of "thinking hats" to view opportunities and options through a variety of perspectives. It is much like putting on another pair of the story glasses described in chapter 4. A group can do this with various members figuratively or even literally wearing colored hats representing the perspectives they are to consider and share. The facilitator wears a blue hat to clarify the objective and rules, encourage all participants to share, and keep everyone on track. Those wearing white hats share facts related to the situation, much like the Story Shaping's Read the Backstory step. Red hats share their immediate gut reactions and ideas. Black hats then approach the problem logically, pointing out problems, barriers, and weaknesses in the ideas. Those wearing yellow hats focus on benefits and look for harmony, while those in green hats encourage the team to probe more deeply, explore new options, and investigate possibilities.[13]

Another suggestion to increase the number of options is simply to get the input of someone with a fresh perspective, especially if that person is an uninterested expert. Smell has always been the most effective of my five senses. As a child, I recognized the distinct, pervasive aroma of different places. They were not usually bad smells, just distinct. If someone would have blindfolded me and taken me to the home of any of my friends, I could have immediately guessed which house I was in by the smell alone. But my house did not have a smell. At least, I did not notice an aroma in my house.

As an adult, I continued to notice this phenomenon. Other houses had distinct smells, but mine had no discernible smell. One day, after my family had moved from one community to another, my son's seventeen-year-old best friend came to visit us in our new home. He walked through the door, sniffed deeply, and called out, "Ah! Smells like an Ehler home!" My immediate reaction was to respond, "What do you mean? Your house smells. Ours does not." Then it hit me. I had grown desensitized to our own smells by their constant presence.

What is true about our sense of smell is also true about our ability to accept the status quo. We tend to accept what is as normal, and it becomes difficult to see other possibilities. So it can help to bring in a fresh "sniffer" when we are stuck. Some people are pros at finding an organization's metaphorical smelly socks or rotten food. Others can locate the hidden door of opportunity embedded in a closet of tradition. We call people in these roles consultants and coaches, and they can bring great value to a decision-making process. At their best, consultants are familiar with relevant solutions but emotionally separated enough from the status quo to give bold, fresh suggestions.[14]

B. REDUCE THE OPTIONS TO A MANAGEABLE NUMBER

Once we have created a list of all the possible options we can imagine, it is time to get the list narrowed down to a manageable size.

This may seem counterproductive. Why go to all the trouble to increase our number of options just to reduce it again? The reason is that imagining options exercises creativity and opens our minds to new possibilities we would not have considered before. But it takes time and effort to evaluate each possibility. The effort required to evaluate and decide among many options can be overwhelming and lead to a paralyzing decision overload.[15] Since detailed analysis works best with a limited group of options, it is wise to select a smaller number for consideration.

Luc de Brabandere and Alan Iny, experts in corporate problem solving for the Boston Consulting Group, laid out an approach in their book *Thinking in New Boxes* that involves five steps:

1. Doubt Everything
2. Probe the Possible
3. Diverge
4. Converge
5. Evaluate Relentlessly

Their step 3, "diverge," aligns with Story Shaping's "raise the number of options," and "converge" corresponds to "reduce the options to a manageable number." They call these essential steps to get people out of "old boxes" of limited thinking. Expanded creativity usually leads to the best solutions, but effective consideration of options requires a limited number.[16] Depending on the situation, between three and seven options allows each to be studied carefully.

The option-reducing process begins with eliminating those that obviously will not accomplish the objective, do not inspire, or do not match your or the organization's ethics and values. Next, consider merging ideas. "And" is often better than "or." See if more than one option has significant overlap or compatibility. Suppose you are considering expanding your restaurant's offerings. One idea may be to offer breakfast. Another is to open an espresso bar. Though these developed as separate ideas, they could be combined for consideration, since espresso drinks go well with a good breakfast.

If a large number of options remain, look for items to study further. For instance, if your restaurant's brainstorming list contains sixty potential new items to add to the menu, pick one or two of each type to run through the rest of the process. Generalized options are difficult to evaluate. Picking specific possibilities is a better test. It can also be beneficial to run through several iterations of the best options.

Another option is to consider a wider range of possibilities. If you are considering opening new locations around a metro area, instead of evaluating three neighborhoods with similar demographics, evaluate a downtown location, one in an established suburb, and one in a new development. This will give you a broader range of results.Once you have selected your options to consider further, write them down with specific descriptions so you can track your findings through the next steps in the process.

C. EVALUATE THE REMAINING OPTIONS

Next, you need to evaluate each item that made your initial cut to see whether it could be the best choice. You can use several tools in this part of the process.

Research. Objective, relevant data often contributes to the best decisions. Good research can produce hard data that guides toward a clear decision between two options. The mobile internet has made this easier than ever. I love trying new foods, but eating at a restaurant I have never seen is risky. Now, when visiting a new city, I can pull out my phone and open Yelp or TripAdvisor to see what unique restaurant has the highest customer reviews. Those few minutes of research usually yield a delicious decision.

Suppose you are starting a new store and need to decide on a location. You find one place for lease at $5,000 per month and another at $10,000. At this point, the first option would seem to be the obvious choice. But you choose to research further. You realize the cheaper facility is located on a side street with little traffic. In your study, you discover the former tenants attempted a business much like the one you want to start but went out of business because their average monthly gross income was just $3,000. You then visit the $10,000 per month location and see it is right on a major thoroughfare and has adequate signage and excellent parking. You check the records and learn the former tenant moved because their business grew too large and they had a new facility custom built. Your research revealed their monthly gross income exceeded $60,000. Even though the lease payment is higher in Option B than in Option A, the math shows clearly that Option B is the better choice. Who would not choose a monthly profit of $50,000 over a loss of $2,000? Well-conducted research can make a big difference.

Depending on the dilemma you face, research can come in different forms and from various sources. Some research is objective and measurable. This includes costs, quantities, censuses, and surveys. You can gather much data from the internet, books, magazines, academic journals, and federal reports. Some organizations compile data. For churches and other ministries, companies such as MissionInsite and Percept gather a large amount of demographic data on local areas, including the relative level of spiritual receptivity among the community's people. This can be useful in determining an outreach approach or in deciding where to launch a new church.

Data drives changes in technology, industry, and commerce in ways that were unimaginable a few decades ago. Have you noticed how many stores now send you coupons for products you buy on a regular basis? They are using data they have obtained about your actual purchases.[17] Authors Chip and Dan Heath warn against falling into "confirmation bias." This occurs when leaders neglect to consider hard data that goes against their assumptions.[18] You may think you know how things actually are, but hard data tells the truth. Obtain objective data whenever possible and applicable.

Other research is difficult to measure yet still important in making decisions. The academic world calls this qualitative research. It can include studying specific people, companies, and groups. Although qualitative research does not produce concrete data, it can provide important insights that quantitative research cannot.[19]

For example, suppose you need to hire a new employee for a key role. You receive many applications from people who have good qualifications (quantitative data), such as high college and high school GPAs, but does that mean they are best equipped to do the job? If the person needs to be able to interact with other people in sales or management, how can you measure that quantitatively? It may be impossible to turn such characteristics into hard data, but calling the potential employees' former supervisors and coworkers will give you far more important insights in determining which candidate will be best for the position.

Overall, be open to learning in formal settings, such as classes and conferences, as well as from informal relationships and models of similar situations. Take the context and history of other cases into consideration before immediately adopting an idea. Lessons learned by others, which you discover through research, can provide valuable insights.

Learn from Other Disciplines. We can learn from fields other than the ones in which we work or with which we are familiar.[20] Many developers have gotten ideas from unrelated disciplines that led to their best products. Let your creative juices flow wherever you go. Attend conferences to get a sense for what is working in other areas that might be adapted to solve your problems. You can also study trends in one field that may precede trends in your own area of concern.

Analyze Likely Trajectories. Once you have researched each option, evaluate the long-term ramifications of the success of each. Be careful how you project the future. Most people tend to exercise trend spotting, which assumes recent trends will continue into the future. Yet trends rarely continue at the same rate for long periods. The housing boom of 2002–2006 in the US is an excellent example. Many who bought investment homes in that period assumed that the rate of price increase would continue indefinitely. Sadly, many lost their fortunes.

Story Shaping proposes an alternate approach called "trajectory prospecting." Rather than assuming trends will continue, it assumes trajectories are a more accurate way to anticipate the future. It avoids the "regression to the mean" fallacy pointed out by Kahneman, which occurs when high performance in a small sample size eventually reverts to normal performance.[21] Trajectories capture the nonlinear, wave-like quality of fashions, fads, and other phenomena.[22] Considering a range of possible outcomes increases their accuracy. More outcomes make trajectory prospecting more complex and time consuming, yet the broader consideration can enable us to make decisions with more confidence. Trajectory prospecting involves a couple of steps.

1. Before trying to predict the future, *plot the trajectory to the current point.* Look for patterns, the length and intensity of cycles, forces that caused trajectory changes in the past, and the shape and direction of the most recent trajectory. Were earlier changes volatile, or has change been consistent? What factors have caused the most significant changes in the past? Are there earlier times similar to the current one?

As examples of plotting past trajectories, see the graphs

showing: (1) a child's growth, (2) the Dow Jones Industrial Average, and (3) the win/loss percentage of the Detroit Tigers.

They vary considerably. It would be dangerous to invest in stocks and expect them to perform like a child's growth chart. Yet we can study the trajectory of the stock market to see how it has been doing, which can influence our investments or decision to buy a home or much more.

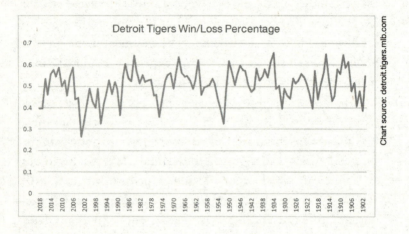

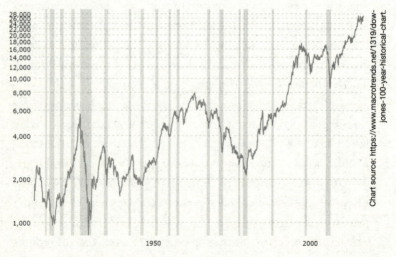

Chart source: https://www.cdc.gov/growthcharts/data/set1clinical/cj41l022.pdf.

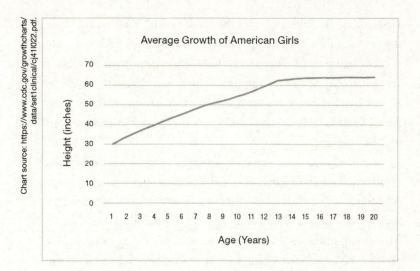

2. Next, *select the most representative prospects.* Rather than prospecting trajectories for every remaining option on your list, select a few that represent the most likely outcomes.

The best approach is often to consider three broadly separated outcomes. For example, if you are considering an investment and have plotted its trajectory to the current point, your first prospect could be that it continues to rise at the same rate as it has recently. You could base a second prospect on earlier downturns, determining about how often they occurred and how far the value dropped. Third, you can look back at the biggest growth cycles and determine when one might happen again. This will give you three realistic, yet variable, prospects to take to the next step.

3. *Look backward from each prospective outcome.* The Heaths and Annie Duke recommend conducting "premortems" by mentally imagining a situation after undesirable outcomes have happened and asking, "What factors led to our failure? What did we do wrong?" Similarly, you can use mental images of success in what

Duke calls "Backcasting" and the Heaths call "Pre-parades," asking yourself, "Why did this succeed?"[23] Looking backward from good or bad possible futures can help pinpoint potential problem areas to avoid. It can also suggest which outcome is more likely. A cost-benefit analysis may assist in evaluating each likely outcome. Options whose outcomes carry high risk but little reward may be eliminated.

Annie Duke recommends a further step quantifying the likelihood of the outcomes and benefits we're prospecting. Although we cannot know future events for sure, we can estimate probabilities. When dealing with financial costs and benefits, we can multiply those by the percentage of likelihood to give an objective weight to each option. For example, suppose you have a temporary job assignment in a city that will keep you there for two years. Should you buy a home or rent? Although house prices will fluctuate, closing costs and realtor commissions usually remain steady over time, with up to 7 percent of the sale price split between the buyer and the seller. You can quantify how much your new home would need to increase in value to offset the expenses of buying and selling. You can then compare that amount to housing market trajectories. (See the chart below.) On average, housing prices across the United States have increased between 2 and 2.5 percent per year. Although some years have seen much higher increases, they are uncommon, and, as we witnessed in 2007–2009, there is always a risk of houses losing value. When you run the numbers, does it make sense to buy a house for your short-term assignment? Unless you plan to hold onto it as a rental property, you will more than likely not earn back the costs of buying and selling a home within a short period. Even a generous 3 percent annual gain will not cover 7 percent in closing costs in two years.

fred.stlouisfed.org, Source: US Census Bureau

Look at Each Remaining Option through Your Intentional Lenses. Carefully evaluate the options and their outcomes to determine which are in line with your or your groups' beliefs, ethics, and values. The intentional lens defines what is right and good, instead of bad and wrong, and what is most important. Eliminate options that conflict with your ethics and values. For instance, your workplace may have an option to make a lot of money that will require lying to the government, but if you believe lying and disobeying the government is wrong, do not consider the option.

Theological Reflection: Although Catching God's Story constitutes the second major step in Story Shaping, it is always wise to reevaluate possible decisions by seeking God's story one more time. Perhaps crafting a new story produced a new awareness to God's work and desire in your situation. We use the same criteria as in Step Two: seeking guidance in Scripture, from the Holy Spirit, and from the Christian community, in that order. Test each option to see whether any Scripture prohibits it. If so, remove it.

See also whether there is a biblical command that is favorable to the option or a biblical example with something relevant to contribute.

Next, note any clear or likely guidance from the Holy Spirit related to each option. Do not be surprised if God speaks while you are trying to craft a new story. In Acts 16, the apostle Paul set out on his second journey. It started with the goal of encouraging and strengthening some of the churches he and Barnabas planted in their first journey. After visiting the established churches, Paul sought to plant more. At first he headed west from Pisidian Antioch toward the province of Asia. Its capital, Ephesus, was the largest city in that part of the world. It probably made sense to Paul's natural reasoning that his mission of spreading the gospel of Jesus to as many as possible would continue best in the largest and most influential city. But Acts 16:6 says they were "kept by the Holy Spirit from preaching the word in the province of Asia." Luke does not tell us exactly *how* the Holy Spirit did that forbidding, but Paul and friends obviously interpreted it as supernatural divine direction. Notice that in this case the Holy Spirit did not give them a clear destination; he just told them where not to go.

Since they were prevented from heading west, Paul and his team tried to go north into Bithynia, but again "the Spirit of Jesus would not allow them" (Acts 16:7). God told them what not to do again, but he did not give specific directions beyond the original command Paul had received at his conversion in Acts 9 and his initial summons to mission in Acts 13:1–3. Paul exercised reason to determine an appropriate place to preach the gospel next, while steering clear of the places God had told him not to go. He headed northwest until he came to the end of the Asian continent, not far from the ancient Greek city of Troy made famous in Homer's *Iliad*. Once he got to the newer port city of Troas, Paul picked up his new friend, companion, physician, and scribe Luke, and he received a vision of a man across the Aegean Sea in northern Greece calling out to him for help. After prayerful, consultation between Paul, Silas, Timothy, Luke, and perhaps others, they reached a clear conclusion: "We got ready at once to leave for Macedonia, concluding that God had called us to preach the gospel to them" (Acts 16:10).

Notice that Paul did not stop moving when he sensed God did not want him to go to Ephesus. He used his reason to keep moving forward and discovered later what God wanted him to do. I have found many times in life and ministry that God's ideas become clear only after I have worked hard using my own creativity and research and consulted with others.

As a youth pastor, I had a desire to reach as many students as possible who were not involved in any church with the good news of Jesus. Some of my friends conducted outreaches on Friday nights in which they would rent inflatable games and do fun activities. These were good events for church youth to invite their non-churched friends to attend. My leadership team and I conducted a lot of research, visited other churches' events, and did creative brainstorming to develop the best Friday night outreach we could imagine. Of course, we prayed along the way, and I felt a peace throughout the process, but I never received a dream, vision, or prophetic word.

We worked hard to make our event as good as it possibly could be. We bought laser tag equipment, built some of our own games and challenges, decked out the facility with black lights and fog machines, got a great team of volunteers in place, and copied hundreds of flyers for our students to distribute at their schools.

I was excited to see what would happen that first night but was disappointed when fewer students showed up for it than usually came to our weekly youth services. Some of the leaders suggested the whole idea was a dud and we should scrap future events. I prayed hard about it. In those prayers, I felt a strong conviction that we needed to try it again. Though there were few guests that first night, two new girls who came had made a commitment to follow Jesus. One later became a key leader in our youth ministry. I knew the event had been worth it for them, and I also knew God's still small voice was not telling me to cancel future events.

The next month we had three times as many people as the first month. The vast majority of the kids had no church involvement of any kind, and when I gave a short explanation of the gospel, more than twenty gave their lives to Jesus. This happened month after month, and many of the kids whose first experience ever in a church building was at one of our Friday night events came back the following Tuesday for our youth service. Attendance at the youth service began to grow, as did the sense of the presence of the Holy Spirit. Before long, nearly every week students who had never set foot inside a church before were responding to the message and coming forward to receive Christ, exclaiming, "What is this? I have never felt anything like this before. I need this Jesus you are talking about! I can tell God is here!"

God's plans often become clearer as we go through the decision-making process, so it is always good to take another opportunity for theological reflection before making a final decision. Be sure that what you plan to do does not violate Scripture or its principles. Test anything that seems to be the Spirit's guidance. Consult with wise fellow believers when it is appropriate.

On your list of options, note your findings after theological reflection. You may need to eliminate some options. Other items may lack support from Scripture, the Spirit, or the church. Note the lack of clear direction and weigh that in your final decision, especially if other options do have biblical support.

D. MAKE A DECISION

The best option may now be clear. Perhaps the process of evaluating options eliminated all but one choice. Even if not, you must make a decision. You cannot predict the future, and the best choice will not always be clear. Working this process prayerfully can enable you to decide with confidence, even in the face of uncertainty.[24] James tells us to ask God for wisdom (James 1:5), which is the key skill needed to decide. A timely, decisive choice, even when you are not a hundred percent sure it will work, is usually key to long-term success. In fact, studies have shown that the fastest growing companies usually have decisive leaders.[25] Andy Stanley is the founding pastor of North Point Community Church near Atlanta, one of America's largest. He calls the leader who craves certainty before deciding an "imposter shepherd" who can lead people in the wrong direction. He said, "I don't have to have everything figured out before I lead out."[26] If you always wait until you are sure, you will never do anything.

Review the steps you took to reduce the number of options. Consider which option came out on top more often than others. If no clear option stands out, put the highest priority on the theological reflection step and the second highest priority on the cost-benefit step. Many Christians will have a sense of peace as they prayerfully reflect on the choice.

Sometimes you will not have time to reflect on these steps again or even to do so carefully a first time. When you need to choose fairly quickly among a large number of options, try using the approach Herbert Simon developed called "satisficing."[27] Get an image in your mind of what you wanted before beginning the evaluation steps and select the first option that comes close to that image and is good enough.[28] My wife and I have two different ways to shop for greeting cards. It is important for her to know she has picked the best card possible for the person she wants to honor. She gave me five birthday cards one year because she could not decide between them. I try to use Simon's approach and envision basic characteristics about an appropriate card for the person who will receive it before I walk into the Hallmark store. I select the first card that is "good enough" by that criterion. Although it is possible I am missing a better card among the thousands I did not read, the decision is sufficient. I will assume the card's recipient would rather have the extra forty minutes with me that it would have taken for me to examine all the other cards. This "good enough" approach is an excellent way to reduce the agony and energy expended when you have a significant, but not all-important, decision to make with many possible choices.

Making a decision that impacts only you spares the challenge that comes from a decision that affects a family, a group, or an organization. When a team works through a process of evaluating options, consensus may or may not come. Americans often default to democratic resolution. Sometimes a majority vote is fine, but other times a vote may not yield the best decision. An organizational structure may determine whether a vote is the ultimate selector or whether a leader is free to make the final decision. When it is the leader's responsibility, the wisest leaders seek the best outcome for everyone involved after considering as many internal and external factors as possible.[29]

Many great leaders in the Bible faced the fear that accompanies the responsibility of decision making. After serving as Moses's assistant for years, Joshua found himself in charge of leading the whole nation of Israel into a land God had promised to them but that was still occupied by enemy armies. He had reason to be afraid, but God repeated the words, "Be strong and courageous," to him three times while giving Joshua the promise the nation would enter and take all the Promised Land (Joshua 1:1–9). Not all of Joshua's decisions were wise decisions,[30] but, ultimately, he became a brave leader and the people of Israel conquered Canaan. So decide. Be strong and courageous, and trust God to bring about the best outcome possible (Romans 8:28).

E. DEVELOP A PLAN TO ENACT THE DECISION

The final part of writing a new story is developing a plan to implement the decision. This is often uncomplicated. Some decisions require only one person to take one action. But revising the structure of a company or the ministry plan of a church may require a significant planning process. Even conflict resolution will require some planning to make your decision take hold. Here is a simple approach to developing a plan.

1. Start at the End

Nearly every time you get into your car, you do so because you have a place in mind you want to go. Whether it is to buy groceries, go to work, or visit a friend, your purpose defines your destination, and that purpose should drive your journey. Begin your planning process by writing down everything you can think of that should be in place for enacting your decision. Format is not important at this point because your creativity should be free to flow.

2. Identify Critical Components

Go through the list you just made and identify those elements of the destination and the journey that are critical. Begin determining which elements are dependent on others and which elements must be accomplished before others. Save those that are not as important for the more detailed final plan.

3. Develop Steps for Implementation

Structure the key components into manageable steps. There may be only a few for some decisions, while a strategic plan for a large organization may have hundreds. Sometimes a diagram can help display and track steps. In complex planning, a storyboard can help. Get a pad of sticky notes and list each element and related task on a separate note. Put the notes on a board or wall in relationship with the others. Put those needing to be completed before others to the left with those following them to the right. You and your planning team can move these around until you have a plan that looks like it will work well to make your decision happen. Once you have identified all major steps, record them.

4. Select Responsible People

Determine who will be responsible for each step and how many other people will be needed to carry out the plan. You can recruit these people later as part of Telling the Story unless they are part of the planning team. In a complex plan, a job description and/or list of responsibilities and resources can be very helpful.

5. Finalize the Details

When dealing with a larger group, a written plan is likely needed so everyone understands their part. With simpler decisions or smaller groups, such as you and your spouse, you can do this step verbally. Just be sure the plan is clear enough that everyone understands their part in carrying it out.

You may have entered step 3, Craft a New Story, with a general idea of the end goal you want to reach or no idea at all. Either way, the process can yield a good decision. Expand your number of options through creative brainstorming, then reduce the number of options and evaluate the ones that remain. After that, you are ready to decide, and that decision may include a detailed plan. Once you have completed this plan, it will be time to tell your newly crafted story.

CHAPTER **EIGHT**

STEP 4: TELL THE NEW STORY

Far too many excellent stories are never told. Far too often we make a decision but never see its fruit because we fail to act to bring it about. Far too many relationships have returned to conflict because those involved did not follow through on what they had agreed to do.

The final step of Story Shaping—making your decision happen—is the whole reason to start the process. This takes effort. The factors involved in telling your new story may include:

- Determining who needs to hear the story
- Deciding how to tell the story to motivate listeners to embrace it
- Acting to make the story a reality
- Proofreading the story by evaluating it regularly to see whether it needs to be shaped again

You may be tempted to second-guess your decision, but like Julius Caesar's decision to cross the Rubicon River and take his army to Rome, you are best served by focusing your energy and effort on how you will implement it, rather than by agonizing over other choices you could have made.[1]

A. DETERMINE WHO NEEDS TO HEAR THE STORY

Those most affected by a decision need to be aware of it and its impact on them. Many families, companies, churches, and even governments have suffered needlessly because their decisions and accompanying reasons were not clearly communicated. In some cases, a new story will yield a much better result if those affected have an opportunity to speak into the final product.

In our digitally connected world, verbal conversation may be less and less common, but major decisions are usually best shared face-to-face. Select a time and setting free from distraction that allows time to not only explain the decision but also to discuss it.

B. BE CAREFUL HOW YOU TELL THE STORY

The difference between the year's biggest Hollywood blockbuster and a career-ending bomb at the bottom of the box-office earnings is not usually the plots of the movies. Instead, how a story is told makes the biggest impact on how it is received. This is true with real-life decisions too. People's acceptance of decisions affecting them requires special story-telling techniques. Here are a few you may want to use.

1. Keep It Simple

The best stories are often simple stories. Think of your favorite movie or novel. Chances are good that it involves a handful of major characters rather than an overlarge supporting cast. Real life is more complicated. You will interact with dozens of people on an average day, but it is difficult to keep track of dozens of characters in a story. It is in the telling that a story gets its power. A documentary on successful novelist Nicholas Sparks's writing was appropriately entitled, "A Simple Story Well Told." Our goal in telling our new story is just that. We want to make it simple enough to be memorable, but well-told enough that those affected want to live it with us.

Although plans may be detailed, people have difficulty remembering complexity. It may be tempting to try to communicate everything about a plan, but a simple, memorable point—perhaps presented creatively as a model or acronym—will increase the likelihood listeners will embrace the change and follow through with it.[2]

Short presentations with clear main points that speak to listeners' needs are best. You do not need to share every detail. Focus on the key elements:

a. Why the change needs to happen
b. How things will improve when the change is made
c. How the change will happen
d. (Possibly) how what people might fear losing will either not be lost or be replaced by something better
e. The listeners' part in making the change happen

2. Start with the Why

People do not embrace change when they fear losing what they value. As leaders learn the lenses of their followers, especially their values, they can explain a change in a way that speaks to what people care about most. Simon Sinek's *Start with Why* showed that marketing and other persuasive messages that start by answering *What?* or *How?* questions were less effective at motivating people than those that started with *Why.*[3] Pointing out the likely long-term wins of a change and the long-term costs of the status quo can help people embrace a new direction.

3. Frame the Plan with a Clear Model

A model can be a great tool to help your listeners understand and remember a change. This is especially helpful with complex plans, such as organizational restructurings, but even a family can use a model to help everyone get a handle on managing time, tasks, and finances. Rick Warren's *Purpose Driven Church* shook the ministry world in 1995 with its clear and simple baseball diamond model for spiritual development. New church attenders start at home plate on their first visit, move to first base when they become church members, second when they develop spiritual disciplines, third when they learn to serve others, and return to home when they make Christ's mission their own and share the good news with others.

Look for a model that can encapsulate your decision. Keep it simple and tie each component to a major aspect of the plan.

4. Use Metaphors

A metaphor is a concept used to represent something else. We use them in communication all the time even though we are not always aware of it. Have you ever said, "I am dead tired"? You were not actually dead, but the idea of a dead person's lack of energy expressed vividly how you felt. Jesus used metaphors on a regular basis. What the Bible calls parables are simply stories that use objects and experiences from everyday life to explain spiritual principles.

The apostle Paul was also a master at metaphors. Most of the words we use today for spiritual concepts are metaphors derived from his letters. Here are several that explain the significance of Jesus's death for us on the cross, with the original literal (nonmetaphorical) meaning explained first.[4]

- Justified (Romans 5:9)—This legal term was used in courts when a judge declared the one under trial as "right," fully in line with the law, regardless of former behavior. *We were guilty sinners, but Jesus's death met the legal requirement for the wrong we had done, so we can be pronounced innocent when we accept him. He justified us.*

- Redeemed (Titus 2:14)—This word was used to denote paying a ransom to free a prisoner or a slave. *We were slaves to sin, held hostage by Satan, until Jesus paid the price to set us free. He redeemed us.*

- Reconciled (Romans 5:10)—This word described a restored relationship, such as a husband and wife remarrying after a bitter divorce. *Our relationship with God had ended until Jesus restored it. He reconciled us to God.*

- Saved (Ephesians 2:8)—People facing death and unable to help themselves, like a person unable to swim and nearly drowning, are *saved* by others able to do what he or she cannot do. *We were doomed to eternity in hell until Christ saved us.*

- Atonement (Hebrews 2:17)—The root of this word originally meant to completely cover or remove something undesirable. *Jesus's death on our behalf removes all sin and its eternal consequences. He atoned for our sin.*

- Made alive (Ephesians 2:5)—The Greeks used this to describe something being born, such as a newborn calf. *We were dead in sin, but we are made alive together with Christ in his resurrection when we believe in him.*

- Adoption (Ephesians 1:5)—One not born into a family becomes a legal member through adoption. *Jesus's death enabled us to be adopted into God's family.*

- Inheritance (Ephesians 1:14)—Land and all associated wealth were passed down in Roman culture from father to son through an inheritance. *As God's adopted children, we await an inheritance beyond imagination when we are with him forever.*

This is only a partial list of the metaphors used to describe our salvation in Christ. Paul and other biblical writers used metaphors because they explain ideas otherwise hard to understand, enhance memory, and convey emotion. When you are trying to implement change in an organization or in a personal relationship, you need to engage understanding, memory, and emotions.

C. MAKE THE STORY A REALITY

Ultimately, telling a new story requires the courageous step of doing what you have decided to do. In the summer before my sophomore year of college, I helped lead a group of high school students from my church on a trip to the Navajo lands of northern Arizona and southern Utah. We took a break from working with Navajo children on Saturday to go swimming in Lake Powell. The sandstone cliffs at its edge drop straight into water more than a hundred feet deep. It looked inviting for a dive, but I was scared. It was not until two boys four years younger than I was climbed the cliffs, dived in, and surfaced with screams of joy that I gained my own nerve to dive. Even then, finally making the decision was scary, but I dove and never regretted it. Since then, there have been several occasions where I hesitated to dive into a decision. Much like the Lake Powell cliff, I knew the water was deep enough to survive the dive, and it would be worth it, but fear and uncertainty threatened to hold me back. It takes courage to experience the exhilaration of a deep dive.

When the time comes to act, be sure all those with parts to play know what they are supposed to do, why they are supposed to do them, and what part they play in the bigger story. Set a clear time to launch the plan, encourage those who need to act to jump in, then celebrate the start of a great story.

Writing a new story is a lot of work. We can wonder whether

anyone will read it. We can wonder whether it will lead to the better ending we desire. It may help to know that the stories of our lives are always being written. Have the courage to dive in even if your story is not perfect.

D. PROOFREAD

The reality is that stories are almost never perfect in their first drafts. Every author knows the value of proofreading and the rewriting that may come with it. Professional writers seek an editor to make their stories as good as possible.

Similarly, consistent evaluation is critical for long-term success in any endeavor. Early monitoring can reveal needed course correction. One of Shane Snow's recommended "smartcuts" is Rapid Feedback.[5] Luc de Brabandere and Alan Iny urge organizations to "reevaluate relentlessly."[6] Churches and organizations can lock themselves into a changeless pattern unless they stop and evaluate. But we must give a decision sufficient time before making changes. New processes are not as efficient or effective as they can be until the people involved develop the skills to handle them intuitively instead of intentionally. Coworkers who have resolved a conflict need to come back together after a period of time to ensure that the resolution really worked.

Unless your decision is a one-time event, continual evaluation will help you improve. Major changes can rob stability and understanding, but good, thorough, regular assessment, especially after an initial launch, can ensure you have set course in the proper direction.

Once you have made progress, be sure to celebrate early wins. Celebration fuels motivation and builds morale. Clear and early wins will also build ownership of the new plan. Celebrations send a message about what matters most and can become launch pads for further improvement.[7] Studies show that workers are 31 percent less likely to quit a job when they work for companies that prioritize recognizing employee performance in tangible ways.[8] Yet even when you win an early victory, adjustments will eventually need to be made. Your team may win the Super Bowl, but that does not mean you are certain to win next year, and since most of the other teams in the league have figured out your offensive strategy and developed defenses to stop it, you need to improve your game continually to stay on top.

So as you read your new story, take time to be sure it is the best story possible. Every story can be shaped further, and eventually every story will need to be reshaped. When that day comes, it is time to restart the Story-Shaping process. The new story you completed before will now be the old story as you seek God's best for your future.

Now that we have seen how Story Shaping works, let us look at how it can be applied in various contexts.

PART
THREE

WHAT
STORY-SHAPING
LOOKS LIKE

CHAPTER NINE

SHAPING YOUR OWN STORY: MAKING PERSONAL DECISIONS

Decisions, decisions. We each make thousands of decisions a day, from what shirt to wear to what route to take to work and what to eat for supper. As we saw in chapter 2, most of these decisions are fine for our brain's intuitive system to handle. But we also encounter decisions that warrant intentional effort and the increased likelihood of God's direction that comes from following a process like Story Shaping.

Remember, your goal in the first step, Read the Backstory, is to determine what is happening, why it is happening, and who is involved. Some decisions deal with the expected. You may seek to repair or improve existing situations, systems, and habits. On other occasions, you face something new. It could be an emerging opportunity, a fresh inspiration, or an urgent but unanticipated crisis. There may not seem to be a backstory, but in reality every opportunity or challenge comes from somewhere. Determining from where and why can help you better understand how to respond to it.

Begin Story Shaping by praying and asking God to guide you in the process, then write down the dilemma you face. A clearly articulated question at this point can bring focus to the rest of the process and keep you on track if it gets complicated or emotional. The next step is to identify what is driving the dilemma. If it is a problem needing correction, what is causing the problem? If you are not sure, consider what factors may be creating the problem. If the dilemma is a new opportunity, what has caused it? What is making you feel that perhaps you should accept it? Remember, you are not trying to decide yet. The goal is to understand the situation so you can take the best next steps.

Most decisions you make will affect other people. List all those your decision will impact. This may include your family, friends, coworkers, or others. Now go back to that list and mark (1) any who should have a voice in the decision-making process and (2) those to notify when you make the decision. For the first group, note when in the process their voice should be heard. If the person is a spiritual mentor, perhaps that person could pray with you and give you wisdom as you seek to Catch God's Story. You may invite others with a stake in the decision to evaluate options for Crafting a New Story. Remember, getting other people involved will increase their acceptance of a decision in the long term, but it will also increase the time required to decide and potentially bring strong emotions or even conflict to the process.

Once you have read the backstory, it is time to Catch God's Story. We always start by seeking guidance in the Bible. Put a priority on clearly applicable commands in the New Testament, then seek parallel examples in the stories of biblical characters throughout the Bible. Sound interpretation and application of biblical principles is essential. If you are not sure the Scriptures you are reading apply to your situation, do not hesitate to seek out a pastor or a spiritual mentor. The next step is to seek the guidance of the Holy Spirit. We looked in depth at how the Spirit can speak in chapter 4. Sometimes a dilemma may be generated by true inspiration (in-Spirit-ation) or a supernatural conviction that something needs to be changed or done. Other times a growing sense of spiritual direction may feel like the slow loading of a detailed photograph on a computer with a poor internet connection. You see blurry colored outlines at first, but as time progresses, the image becomes clearer and clearer. This latter kind of direction may become clear only as you move into Crafting a New Story.

Anytime you sense supernatural direction, test it (1 Thessalonians 5:19–21). Make sure no Scriptures prohibit what you are feeling led to do. Seek confirmation from other Christians. While on some occasions Christians faced nothing but opposition at the beginning of a new idea, then later saw incredible success, it is more often true that seeking wise counselors brings victory (Proverbs 11:14; 15:22; 24:6). Listen to those who are wise and have an intimate relationship with God. Prioritize people who know and love you and those who understand the dilemma or have been through a similar experience. A phone call or a cup of coffee with a few people such as this can make an enormous difference in your future.

You may come to sense God's will clearly, but if not, that does not mean you should not decide. You turn next to step 3, Craft a New Story. As we saw in chapter 5, we want to begin this step by prospecting through an increased number of options. List every possible decision you can make in the dilemma you face. Even include the crazy ideas, in case they inspire better ones. You may want to invite those with a stake in the decision to share their input. Once you have listed all the ideas you can imagine, begin to reduce them to a manageable number, usually three to seven. Eliminate those opposed to your values and ethics. Pull off any that are unworkable or unlikely to produce a good outcome.

Once you have reduced your set of ideas, evaluate each one.

You may need to do further research or talk to people who have tried the options you are considering. You can use some of the other tools I described in chapter 5, such as the premortem and the preparade tools to evaluate the pros and cons of each option through your intentional lenses of beliefs, ethics, and values. A clear favorite may emerge. Remember, even when that does not happen, we can still decide. Sometimes, an initial decision will be tentative, evaluated after a trial period to see whether another way is better. But a decision must be made. Any test runs of a decision will be part of step 4, Tell the New Story. This step includes telling those who need to know about it and doing so in a way that facilitates their understanding and acceptance, especially if the decision will have an impact on their lives.

Here is an example of how you might use Story Shaping to make a career decision. Suppose you are married, have two young children, and enjoy a job within an hour's drive of your parents and your spouse's parents. One day you get a call from a job search firm working on behalf of one of your employer's competitors. The recruiter asks you to apply for a job with a significant increase in responsibility and pay. But the move will take your family across the country to an area you have wanted to visit but have never been able to. How is that for a dilemma?

After praying for God's wisdom and direction, you highlight a few key strands of backstory. The first is your current situation. Your kids are growing up near their grandparents, you know many people in your community, and you have good friends. Although you enjoy your job, you realize you are not likely to be promoted for a long time. Your supervisor will not retire for at least fifteen years, and his supervisor is younger. If one of them were to leave, three of your peers are likely to compete for the position, as will people from your firm's other locations. Therefore, advancement at your current workplace will take a long time and is not certain.

Another strand of backstory is your community's public school system, which is not highly rated. There is a drug problem in the middle and high schools your children are likely to attend. Your current salary does not provide enough to send your kids to private schools.

A final strand of backstory that you notice when you ask, "What is happening?" is the situation of the other company asking you to apply. The director there left her position, and someone recommended you as a good candidate. This strand will generate several "why?" questions that may take some investigation to answer. Why did the former director leave? Why did they ask you to apply? How likely is it they will offer you the position? Will applying for it put your current job at risk if your boss hears you applied?

It is also important during the Read the Backstory step that you examine your interpretive lenses. Start with the intentional lens. What do you believe about your capability to perform the new job? What do you believe about yourself? Do you tie your identity to the place you have always lived, or can you and your family adjust to a new location? The ethics and values layers of the intentional lens have a lot to contribute in a situation like this one. Do you believe it is wrong to move away from your parents and force your children to make new friends? On the other hand, is it wrong to turn down a promotional opportunity that could enable your children to attend better schools? Which do you value more, staying rooted in the community close to your parents or climbing the career ladder and experiencing the adventure of making new friends and discovering new places? Of course, you will be exercising reason throughout this process as you consider which option is best.

The intuitive lens will no doubt affect your outlook. You may desire to move or to stay. Of course, your spouse's and children's lenses may have different prescriptions when viewing this opportunity. Listening to them to gauge whether they share the same beliefs, ethics, values, and desires will be important, since your move will affect them too. You may or may not want to bring your parents and in-laws into conversations at this point.

As you turn to step 2, Catch God's Story, you should begin by consulting any relevant Scripture. Concerns about letting proximity to your parents drive your decision could be tempered by Genesis 2:24, "That is why a man leaves his father and mother and is united to his wife, and they become one flesh." While this passage does not require a cross-country move, it does set you free from being bound to live near your parents or in-laws. However, if one or more parents are dependent widows, 1 Timothy 5:3–8 commands children to provide for them.

Many characters in both the Old and New Testaments moved because of God's calling and uncontrollable circumstances. Abraham moved from Ur to many places in Canaan before heading to Egypt and then back to Canaan. He worked throughout his moves, and God prospered him. Joseph moved to Egypt against his will, but God brought about a good outcome anyway. Moses fled from Egypt to Sinai in fear until God called him back to Egypt to lead the nation of Israel into Sinai and then to the Promised Land. Many biblical characters moved, worked in their new lands, and saw God do great things for and through them. But though these scriptural examples can encourage you that God can do great things if you take a new job, none of them is a clear command of God calling you to move.

You have no doubt been earnestly open to guidance from the Holy Spirit, but now that you have reviewed the relevant Scripture you could find, be especially open to the ways the Spirit can speak. A friend may share something without knowing your situation that helps you decide. Although rare, you may have a dream or a supernatural vision. More commonly for Spirit-led believers today, you may have a strong internal sense that you need to apply for the position. Or you may feel a strong resistance that is more than just fear of making a bad choice. Many Christians use the idea of "peace" in a situation like this. Peace is subtle but very real. As you pray about the opportunity, do you have a sense of peace about applying? Do you have a sense of peace when you consider turning down the position?

The next step in Catching God's Story is to turn to the Christian community. If it is safe to do so, seek the wisdom of spiritual leaders, friends, and others who know you well, as they can bring clarity and possibly mention factors you have not yet considered. One or more may have a sense of divine direction for you. Usually, the objectivity and experience of such people is the greatest benefit. Praying together can be a powerful way of discerning and confirming God's direction.

Next, Craft a New Story. If you have received clear divine direction, that means you need to work out the details. When God's will is not clear, go through the process: (1) expand the options, (2) narrow the number of options to a manageable list, (3) evaluate each remaining option, and (4) make the best decision possible. Remember to first consider who should join you in your decision-making process. Your spouse is a wise person to invite because the decision impacts your spouse and your children. Your parents may not be a good choice because of their bias at possibly losing regular access to their grandchildren. Your boss is definitely out. Depending on their ages, your children may or may not have the objectivity to assist in the decision, even though you should definitely and carefully notify them of the final decision.

It may seem at first that you have only two prospects to evaluate: (1) apply for the new job or (2) keep the old job. But you need to increase your options as much as possible. There are actually many possibilities. You can (3) apply for a different job at a different company or (4) talk to your boss about being approached by the new company and use it as leverage to request a raise. Similarly, you can (5) go to your CEO to discuss the potential for future advancement. You can even (6) start your own business or (7) go back to school for an advanced degree. You can (8) call your best friend from high school you have not seen for ten years and ask how his life is going. You can even (9) change your career field.

The list could go on indefinitely, but you see the point. The higher numbered ideas above may seem to have gotten ludicrous, but you never know when brainstorming will spark a good idea. Perhaps a phone call with your old friend will inspire you to take a risk and change to a more rewarding career. Maybe you had never thought about starting a business, but taking the time to consider it awakened a desire and an awareness of an opportunity. People who take time to dream like this have started some of the world's greatest businesses.

Once your list is as wide as is realistically possible, begin to reduce it to a manageable size for further study. The first step is to eliminate those ideas that will not work, seem distasteful to you, or are not in line with your ethics and values. In your case, it may be that you do not have the credit or desire to start a business. That idea comes off the list. Perhaps at this stage of life with kids at home, going back to college is not financially feasible. But you do decide to call your old friend on the list. It may not lead to anything in your career, but it will at least be good to catch up. That leaves you with seven ideas: (1) Apply for the new job, (2) stay with the old job, (3) apply for a similar job at a different company, (4) talk to your immediate boss about a raise, (5) talk to your CEO about long-term opportunities, (6) call your old friend, and (7) change careers.

Although seven ideas is a manageable number, consider

merging ideas to shrink the list further. You can put numbers 4 and 5 together in a single conversation with your CEO or immediate supervisor. Perhaps 6 and 7 are related, because you have been curious about your friend's career and how fulfilling it might be. That leaves you with five prospects to evaluate more thoroughly. Let's shift these prospects to letters here to keep them straight:

a. Apply for the new job
b. Stay at your current job
c. Apply for similar jobs at different companies
d. Meet with your CEO
e. Call your old friend and consider a new career

Now it is time to (a) research, (b) analyze trajectories, and (c) reflect theologically on each.

Researching prospect A, applying for the new job, could involve searching online for information about the financial health of the company and its corporate culture. You could also research life in the city to which you would move. What are homes and schools like? Are there recreational opportunities you would enjoy? If you know anyone who has worked for the company or lives in the area, a phone call or coffee conversation would provide excellent insight. (Yes, a macchiato can count as research.) Prospect B does not require research, since it involves the job you already have. Prospect C, applying for a similar job at a different company, is a form of research itself. Even if you don't end up taking another position, viewing job search websites and talking to corporate recruiters can better inform you about what your job is worth and give you ammunition for negotiating a raise at your current company or arguing for a good salary at the new one. Talking to your CEO, prospect D, may provide insight that your future with the company is more promising than you imagined.

It may also be that this kind of conversation with your CEO puts your career at risk. The preliminary step of research for this option may be to ask coworkers how the boss has received their career conversations. Was the boss open to discussion and straightforward about future prospects, or were your coworkers chastised or penalized for broaching the question? If they experienced the latter, a conversation may not be wise. But many leaders appreciate an employee with a pending offer approaching them before accepting the new position. Finally, prospect E, calling your old friend to discuss a career change, counts as research too and might be aided by completing a career interest survey or researching jobs you find interesting.

As you begin researching options, suppose you find prospect A, the new city, has pros and cons. The cost of living is much higher and the schools are not as much better as you'd thought. A Starbucks visit with a former employee of the company who now works for your employer reveals their culture is more toxic than your current workplace. With so many people leaving, it is not surprising they are offering you more money.

Of course, you know about prospect B, staying at your current job; however, a friend encourages you to meet with your CEO, prospect D. You decide it is worth the risk to tell your CEO about the phone call from the headhunter and other job openings you discovered through prospect C. In that conversation, your CEO shares how much you mean to her and the company, and she offers you a raise that would cover the tuition of private school for your children. That would make a great end to your story, but you still have prospect E to consider. More than just a chat with an old friend, you learn during it about a great opportunity not as far away in a healthy company that features fulfilling work and strong future opportunities.

Your reasonable options are down to two. The cross-country

move of prospect A is no longer appealing. Prospect B won't happen, because your CEO has offered you a promotion as a result of prospect D. The question is will you take it or will you pursue the position your friend told you about? We'll call these narrowed down opportunities 1 and 2. Wisdom would call for prayer and more research into 2's viability to see whether it is as good as your friend believes. Let us assume your research into your friend's recommendation leads to a phone call with the CEO there, who invites you for an interview and then offers you an even better raise. The community and schools are attractive, the corporate culture is appealing, and both your parents and your in-laws would be less than three hours away, enabling regular weekend visits.

Look next at the trajectories of 1 and 2. Although both seem good right now, your current company has not seen significant growth for years, while the company in 2 has recently become the market leader. The firm also is ahead in research and development, and you love the direction in which it is heading. It can be good to do a premortem or a preparade here. Envision the end of your career as you retire from each of the two positions. Which vision brings more fulfillment? Is there something special about staying rooted in your community and church, or will it be better to have risen to VP of the other organization?

Finally, you return to theological reflection one more time. Perhaps God's voice is becoming clear in the process to you or your spouse. Bringing your children into the conversation at this point might be wise. One company may have practices that are out of line with your ethics or the Bible's.

Now it is time to decide. Some uncertainty may remain, but you should be equipped to make the best decision possible under the circumstances. You ask your children what they think, and they are excited about the move to the new community. Both the current and long-term trajectory of prospect 2 is better. The best decision is clear. Yet you were not considering or even aware of that opportunity when the first phone call came. Had you not taken the time and effort to craft a new story and expand options, you never would have known about it.

The next step is to develop your plan. In this case, it probably includes getting your house ready to sell, notifying your employer of your departure, finding a place to live in the new community, and saying farewell to friends.

Step 4, Tell the New Story, involves determining how to tell the people you need to tell. The way you speak to your boss and CEO after they had offered you a raise can temper resentment. Helping your parents and in-laws see the benefits of the move might ease the pain of having to drive a few extra hours to see their grandkids. Of course, taking action is the key to making it all happen. With a move of this magnitude, evaluating the decision will differ significantly from evaluating smaller or more reversible decisions, but it will be important to do so. It could involve listening to your children and spouse to allay their fears and integrate as many of their desires as possible in the move and your life in the new city.

This vignette gives you an idea of how you can use Story Shaping to make a decision. The extra effort of Story Shaping can yield real, sometimes unexpected, benefits to you and others involved. A simple gut reaction or weighing the pros and cons of only immediately apparent options often won't lead to the best outcome. The range of decisions you make in a lifetime is enormous, and not every outcome will be clear and successful, but approaching major decisions intentionally and humbly can lead to a better future.

CHAPTER **TEN**

SHAPING OUR STORY: MAKING ORGANIZATIONAL DECISIONS

I have the incredible privilege of serving as dean of Southeastern University's Barnett College of Ministry and Theology. Like many of the Assemblies of God's regional universities, Southeastern was started in the mid-1930s as a three-year Bible school to train ministers and missionaries. In 1950 the school moved to its current location in Lakeland, Florida, then began offering four-year bachelor's degrees. By the 1970s, Southeastern expanded beyond just ministry degrees, and the school grew to nearly 1,000 students, where it stayed until the late 1990s.

By that time, deferred maintenance had left the campus in a homely state. Finances were tight, and the lack of growth for decades had robbed morale and momentum. The board of trustees knew a turnaround would require decisive action, so they took a risk in selecting the next president.

Dr. Mark Rutland had successfully rescued Calvary Assembly in Orlando through his dynamic preaching and leadership. He arrived at Southeastern and led a strategic change process that started with reading Southeastern's backstory. The school had many good elements: a sincere spiritual atmosphere, quality faculty and staff who deeply loved students, and supportive churches around the region. But he quickly diagnosed that the school's limited funds were not being spent in ways that could fuel growth.[1]

Rutland and the leadership team sought God and began to craft a new story to increase financial and academic health. Rutland recognized that leading change required credibility, and he felt the best way to do that was to be very visible. He committed to preach 80 percent of the chapel services and to begin traveling regularly to raise awareness of the school as well as donations. The leadership team developed a courageous, multistage plan that started with the hard decision to shut down some programs to divert the money they consumed into areas more likely to generate revenue, including marketing, enrollment recruiting, and facility facelifts. Part of this initial stage included informing the university's employees and supporters that it would be a while before salaries could increase. Everyone would have to tighten their belt buckles for a season until increased enrollment could bring in enough tuition to reward their faithfulness. The second phase would involve program expansion, including launching master's degrees, adult degree completion programs, major events to bring guests to the revitalized campus, and, eventually, online education.

As Rutland told this new story to staff and faculty, not everyone was convinced the sacrifice would be worth it. Some chose to go elsewhere. Others had to leave because of the programs being shut down, but building new dormitories and renovating the 1950s-era buildings in a beautiful new Mediterranean-style architecture got people's attention. The new enrollment counselors brought in more students. Rutland's preaching around the country brought new awareness. Things began to turn.

Within just a few years, Southeastern's growth put it on the map. Southeastern College became Southeastern University. When so many small Christian colleges were fighting to survive, Southeastern's enrollment tripled in just eight years.

Yet that astounding run plateaued, and Mark Rutland felt led to accept an offer to take the presidency of Oral Roberts University in early 2009. Everyone familiar with Southeastern's incredible story wondered who could possibly replace Rutland as president. A painful, nearly two-year-long search process ensued that included division at nearly all levels, a loss of hope and momentum, and a 20 percent enrollment drop.

After the first search team failed to find an appropriate candidate, a local pastor with national influence, Wayne Blackburn, stepped in to restart the search. The new committee quickly settled on a candidate the first committee had considered but passed over. Dr. Kent Ingle had served as dean of the College of Ministry at Southeastern's sister school, Northwest University, for six years after successfully pastoring churches in the Los Angeles and Chicago metro areas.

Great anticipation accompanied Ingle's interview with all the faculty and staff. Of course, the first question asked was, "What is your vision for the university?" Ingle's response shocked them all. "I can't tell you my vision because I don't know you. Until I understand the potential of the people, I can't possibly envision the potential of the organization."[2] Although he did not use the terminology, he knew he needed to read Southeastern's backstory first. The trustees recognized the wisdom of this response and offered Ingle the position. After a speedy move from Seattle, he followed through on his promise by launching the largest listening campaign in Southeastern's history. He and his wife invited groups of faculty and staff to their home and had them share both what they loved about the school and what they felt needed to be changed.

This approach of listening first may have held growth back initially, but it increased Ingle's credibility and allowed him and the new leadership team to discover the school's strengths to retain as a foundation for future growth. Many of the same healthy elements Rutland had discovered still characterized Southeastern. Many other aspects of the school, especially its campus and reputation, were much healthier than they had been in 1999. But Ingle's leadership team learned through their listening that some things needed to change if the school was going to grow to the next level. Ingle's research and prayerful reflection led him to develop what he now calls Framework Leadership. The leadership team set six frameworks to determine what would be the priorities for the future. Any idea that did not fit in one of these frameworks was dismissed. The new story was crafted, and it was time to tell it. The time spent listening meant employees and stakeholders trusted his leadership, and they were ready to embrace the change they knew needed to come.

Ingle recognized change needed to come quickly, and his Urgent Framework determined budget, systems, and governance. Rather than banking on growth due to his own charisma, Ingle released leadership to others and launched shared governance. He put a priority on discovering the right people from both within and outside the school. The Innovative Framework drove creation of new program ideas, including church-based extension sites that allowed ministry students to get degrees while serving churches across the country. College football is second only to Jesus in the South, and the launch of Fire Football more than paid for itself with many tuition-paying students coming to the school to play.

In less than two years, enrollment had passed the peak of the previous administration. Launching new degree programs and expanding online, dual-enrollment, and extension site education fueled increasing growth. Southeastern's campus continued to expand, and, at the time of this writing, just seven years after Ingle's arrival, enrollment at the school is nearly ten thousand students, more than quadruple what it was when he came.

Although I had not yet fully developed my model of Story Shaping or even visited Southeastern before Mark Rutland or Kent Ingle arrived, this school's amazing growth over the last twenty years shows the model in action. Many well-meaning new leaders arrive at a school, church, business, or other institution with a goal of leading growth and health but instead see decline, opposition, and discouragement. Existing organizations often fail to make change when it is needed. Other groups make decisions that impair their mission rather than moving things forward. These failures often occur because organizations and their leaders skip one or more of the four steps of Story Shaping.

Many aspects of Story Shaping's four steps play out in an organization as they do with individuals, but having many people involved increases the challenge at every level. The first question to ask is, "Who makes the decision?" There are four common organizational decision-making approaches:

1. The senior leader makes a unilateral decision.
2. All members (or affected individuals) vote.
3. A group of representatives votes on behalf of all.
4. The senior leader takes a poll and other factors into consideration, then makes a decision he or she feels is best for the organization.

Legal guidelines may direct which of these approaches you can take. Many corporations have specific bylaws or policies that determine when a decision must be approved by a vote of the governing board or all members. Some organizations have rules that put decision-making responsibilities on an individual.

When no policies direct the approach to decision making, each of these options has strengths and weaknesses to consider. A unilateral decision is quick and clear. A senior leader with acknowledged authority can ensure everyone moves forward in the same direction. Just because a single individual makes the final decision does not mean that person does not listen to others or consider their concerns. Many leaders intentionally convene a group that represents a variety of perspectives in a process like Story Shaping in order to gain as broad a perspective and as much good data as possible before deciding. But there is a risk of discontent when some disagree with the leader's decision. Of course, when one person decides, there is also a risk of selfish or unethical decision making rather than what is best for the organization.

A vote of all involved ensures everyone's voice has equal value and that the desire of the majority happens. This may sound wonderful—fair and equitable—to those who value a democratic system of government. The weakness of the vote, though, is that not every person has equal wisdom, perspective, or decision-making ability. Individual self-interest usually motivates people more than what is best for the organization. While there are occasions when a vote is the right way to decide, it does not always yield the best outcome. Large votes also have the cumbersome challenge of letting everyone know about the vote and the real issues involved. Voting is much easier now with internet applications, but individuals are not likely to read all the background information before casting an electronic ballot.

Representative democracy has been the American solution to this challenge since our founding as a nation. People elect representatives from their areas who gather to hear evidence and debate issues before casting ballots. In theory, this approach provides the best of both worlds. Power is not in the hands of one person, those voting gain an understanding of the issues they decide on, and there is an equitable balance of representation. A representative approach solves many weaknesses of the first two approaches, but an elected individual voting in a way that those who elected the person would want is not guaranteed. There is also no guarantee that voters will fully understand the issues or the perspective of the senior leader.

The fourth model works well when a selfless, wise leader is at the helm. All voices have an opportunity to speak. The decision-maker can consider all relevant information. That person usually has the unique perspective and responsibility to decide on behalf of others. Asking key questions is very important. Getting input from a poll and not a vote lets others know their opinions matter. The risk of wrong motives remains, but organizations can put methods of accountability in place. This approach may not always be the best approach to decision making, but it often yields good decisions.

The first Story-Shaping step of Reading the Backstory is nearly always more complex in an organization than with an individual. Many new key leaders enter an organization assuming they know what is best. Some saw significant success at another organization and assume that what worked well there will work in the new location. I have seen pastors arrive at a new congregation and immediately implement the ministry systems, programs, and styles of their former churches in their new church without taking time to learn what has been done in the past—what worked, and what did not work. The copycat approach is not guaranteed to fail, but not taking time to listen and learn creates unnecessary risks.

Aspects of an organization's backstory that a new leader should seek to read include the following:

Mission—Why does the organization exist? What is it supposed to accomplish? Although most organizations were founded with specific missions, those who work for these organizations do not always consciously embrace the stated missions. Most American businesses have profit making as a key element of their mission statements, but not all their employees go to work thinking, "I hope my company makes a big profit today." Although they want the company to succeed enough to cover their paychecks, they may avoid the extra work that could increase income. But if they are also corporate stockholders, they might work more to fulfill the company's mission—and make a bigger profit.

Many church attenders hold different mission statements in their minds than the one posted on the church website. They may believe the mission of the church is to worship God the way they always have in the same building they always have with the same people they always have. Many pastors will say their church's mission is to grow through people coming to faith in Christ. Growth and new people fulfill the pastor's definition of mission effectiveness, but that could destroy the attenders' idea of the church's mission. The two "mission statements" are in direct opposition even though they are held by people in the same congregation.

Reading the backstory of an organization involves discovering both what the mission statement *should be* and what various people involved *believe it is*. If you discover a disparity between perceived missions, be sure to keep it in mind throughout the Story-Shaping process. Changing the perceived mission must become part of the plan, and the new story must be told in a way that helps as many as possible to embrace it.

Characters—Another important part of reading the old story includes listening to the most influential people in the organization. Many of these people may hold positions of power, but not all do. Some people express their opinions loudly and are able to shape how others view circumstances, actions, and other people. Find these people early in the process. Be sure to take time to listen to them to determine how they read the backstory. When making decisions or planning as a team, it is best to get as many of these people on the team as possible, especially those who believe in the organization's mission and are willing to make changes to see the mission fulfilled.

Values—We saw earlier that values are a key layer of the intentional story-reading lens. You will need to determine what people care most about in any decision affecting the organization. More than likely, people hold a variety of values. They may conflict. Some value tradition and stability, while others value creativity and trendiness. You will likely discover values that differentiate this organization from others with similar missions. Focus on them. Some may need to change. Some may be ancillary. Some may help people buy into changes if you can demonstrate how the new story will better embrace those values.

Systems—Efficient organizations are intentional about how they do things. Systematic handling of repeated tasks speeds up completion and reduces errors. Even if unintentional, every organization has systems. Depending on the type of decision you are making, it may be important to discover and evaluate the systems in place. When arriving as a new senior leader, it is very important to determine the key systems related to your organization's mission. How is the main mission accomplished? How are funds handled? How do leaders direct and manage the workers? How are facilities maintained? Improving systems can increase profitability and quality.

Culture—Every organization has a unique culture that includes values and systems and much more. Culture determines how tasks are done and how people relate to one another. Culture can be difficult to quantify, but it has a big impact. If you have worked in a similar job at more than one organization, you probably noticed the culture change quickly. Culture is created, both intentionally and unintentionally, by leaders, long-term participants, historical practices, and values. Context itself can significantly affect an organization's culture.

One key element of culture is leadership style. Some organizations have a top-down authoritarian leadership structure. The military, for example, functions with senior officers giving commands to junior officers, who give orders to enlisted personnel. There is no democratic vote. Many companies also function well with an authoritarian leadership culture. Some churches have lay people who follow the pastor's direction without question. Yet people in other organizations expect a voice if not a vote in all major decisions. Many people consider leadership culture an ethical issue. Some lower-level employees may think it is wrong if they do not have a voice in company policy, while their leaders may view it as wrong for employees to complain and ask for a vote.

If you are new to a senior leadership position, try to discover your organization's recent leadership culture. Change may be appropriate, but expect opposition if you try shifting from less control at the highest level to more control. If you need to make a decision and your group has been comfortable with authoritarian leadership in the past, you probably are fine to walk through Story Shaping alone, so long as you have the knowledge and resources you need. But people are not likely to accept such a decision if the organization has had a democratic leadership culture.

Context—A final aspect of the backstory you may need to read is your organization's context. This includes the surrounding community as well as other organizations seeking to provide a similar product or service. Many churches fail to reach their communities because they do not take time to know and understand the people in them. What do they want and need that you can provide? How can you best let them know about what you offer? What is likely to motivate them to visit you?

An organization seeking to expand into a new area may already know its own culture, values, systems, and mission, but it is wise to understand the new context. What are the values and cultural influences there? How do they differ? How should any differences drive your methods, styles, marketing, and outreach?

Once you have grasped the mission, characters, values, systems, culture, and context of an organization, you are ready to address the specific dilemma. The other elements of Reading the Backstory that determine what is happening and why take center stage. Depending on the depth and breadth of the dilemma, this step might involve a great deal of research and intense listening exercises. Apply one or more of the methods laid out in chapter 5 to discover what is healthy and should be retained, what needs to be removed or repaired, and what attempts have been made in the past at resolving the dilemma. Wrap up the Reading the Backstory stage by writing a statement summarizing what you want to achieve by the end of the decision-making process.

Now it is time to Catch God's Story. Start with a biblical study of any texts directly applicable to your dilemma. Next, look for principles from narrative parts of Scripture that may have ramifications for your situation. Be open to any special revelation that may come from dreams, visions, prophecies, or an internal sense of God's leading, but always test it. Seek God's best from the larger Christian community as well. Sometimes a sense of God's confirmation can come as a strategic team wrestles through the planning process. Experienced experts can bring wisdom, or even a sense of divine guidance, to teams. External help may be useful as you seek to Catch God's Story, or during step 3, Craft a New Story, or in both.

As always, you will emerge from Catching God's Story in one of three situations:

1. You *know* what God wants you to do.
2. You think you may know what God would have you do.
3. You have no idea whether God has anything specific to say about this situation.

If the first applies, jump to the planning step. If you are not sure or have no idea, then begin to Craft a New Story.

Chapter 7 presents several tools to aid you in expanding the number of options you consider, then reducing and evaluating them. Most are designed for group use, seeking the broadest representation of voices to speak into the process while you obtain data and evaluate options. You can solicit ideas from people through group brainstorming, surveys, storyboarding, looking at other organizations in your field, studying other fields for parallel ideas, and lateral thinking exercises. Nothing builds team spirit like putting on colored thinking hats does.

Even when the final decision will be made through an organization-wide vote, it is usually best to have a smaller group narrow the options, evaluate them, and make a recommendation. But people often get attached to their suggestions and lose objectivity. Groups larger than seven to twelve are cumbersome to manage. It's best if the group that narrows options is not too large and made up of people who have broad expertise in the field, the trust of others in the organization, and a genuine concern for the organization's welfare.

As we saw in chapter 7, the reduction team can eliminate ideas that will not work or oppose the organization's values. They can also consider merging ideas when appropriate, selecting a reasonable number of solid ideas to take to the research and evaluation phase.

It might be wise at this point to bring in a consultant or talk to similar organizations that have tried similar solutions, if you can find them. Run everything through the intentional lens layers of beliefs, ethics, and values to be sure any remaining ideas are appropriate for your organization. Of course, seek to Catch God's Story one last time and be sure nothing remains out of line with Scripture or what you believe the Holy Spirit might be saying.

Then make the decision in the method most appropriate for your organization. If that is by voting and you have more than one good option left, an election between them may work. Other organizations have bylaws requiring a yes or no vote on one option at a time. Either way, be sure to adhere to your governing documents.

The final part of Crafting a New Story is creating a plan to implement the decision. Even when a decision is reached by a vote, it is not usually best to create a plan with a large group. Certain individuals have the temperament, talent, and skills to create good plans. Perhaps an appropriate person could be selected to create a draft plan and submit it to a guiding panel, which can then point out improvements to ensure every step of the process is likely to lead to excellent implementation.

Once the plan is developed, leaders need to Tell the New Story. The elements of this step described in chapter 8 are especially important in large organizations where people are not likely to want change. All those affected will need to hear about the decision, so communicating it clearly and simply is critical. The organization's mission and values should drive how the story is told.

Although every dilemma and organization is unique, here are some common scenarios that may be confronted when it's time to Tell the New Story.

1. **Those most affected want to see change and will support the decision**—It is wonderful to lead a group that wants to be led and is eager to make changes the leader says are

essential to the mission. Often people accept simple decisions and move forward in unity. In such cases, it is still best to be clear on why the change is coming and how it will affect those involved. Asking people to support the change and work to make it happen will likely increase ownership. Without delay, share a simple, clear explanation and plan to let everyone know what is happening and why.

2. **Significant change is needed that will require ending a long-cherished aspect of the organization**—Many decisions require change that is uncomfortable. Someone once said that the only person who likes change is a wet baby. When people choose what organizations to join or what events to attend, they typically make their decision based on personal preference, beliefs, ethics, and values. When a decision affects any of these, people may not be happy. People's story-reading lenses have a real impact on how they interpret a situation. Sometimes changes involve personnel. If long-time, much loved employees are laid off, whether for performance, financial reasons, or program changes, people will be sad to see them go, but they may also view the decision as an ethical violation. ("It is wrong to fire them!") The decision may produce opposition and weakened morale. It is critical to plan carefully how you tell the new story. Start by recognizing what will be lost when the decision is implemented. Consider how those affected will view what is lost. Will they see it as an issue of ethics or values or beliefs? Next, clarify the values, ethics, or beliefs that the change will uphold. Not every decision will have a positive outcome that can be used to persuade others to accept it. Some decisions must happen because of financial limitations or other unpleasant realities. Most

of the time, explaining that you are making the best decision that can be made under the circumstances will boost your credibility as a leader and bring greater acceptance of the change. Even if there are practical, legal, or structural reasons and you cannot tell the whole story, it is best to explain as clearly as possible why you made the decision, how it will affect them, and what they need to do now for the best outcome possible.

3. **Factions in the organization form in support of and in opposition to the decision**—In this case, some groups wear different lenses, often involving the ethics and values layers. Two groups may have different ideas about what is "right" and "wrong." One group may have values that conflict with the values of the other. We can see this in action by watching the US Congress or cable news networks. Switching between Fox News and CNN displays opposing perspectives and values. When you make a decision you know some will like and others will hate, it is best to plan for ways to tell the story to both groups, perhaps separately at first if you have that option. When you speak to all at once, it may be best to focus on the organization's mission and shared values. Clarify any misunderstandings the opposition may hold. Share a vision for a better future resulting from the decision. An appeal for involvement may give those initially opposed to a decision a reason to work hard to make it happen. It is not always possible to have everyone celebrate a decision, but putting effort into telling the new story well can increase the likelihood of long-term health and unity.

The final part of Telling the New Story, proofreading, is especially critical in an organization. Evaluate the decision regularly. Did it accomplish what it was supposed to? Did it solve the problem? Do you need to tweak how it is working? Are the right people doing the right things the right way for the best long-term benefit? Ask these kinds of questions regularly. If you make a major change in strategy or processes, systematize your evaluation. Determine how often the evaluation should happen. One-time decisions will not require this level of critical analysis, but it is still important to look back and see how well they worked. Even evaluate the decision-making process itself. What can we do better the next time our organization must make a decision?

As we saw in chapter 3, Acts 15 features an excellent example of a group decision that integrates the steps of Story Shaping. Acts traces the growth of the church starting in Jerusalem, spreading through Judea and Samaria, and then moving beyond those Jewish-dominated regions to Antioch in Syria by chapter 10. Many who came to believe in Jesus were Gentiles, not Jews, and it did not take long before a disagreement erupted over what non-Jewish believers needed to do to become Christians.

The apostles Paul and Barnabas and the Christians in Antioch believed Gentiles needed only to believe in Jesus to become Christians. They felt Gentiles should not be circumcised, because that would be trying to earn God's favor through the Jewish law, not the faith that Christ prescribed. But some Pharisees who had become Christians disagreed. They believed that becoming a Christian meant becoming a Jew, and this required following all of the law, including circumcision. Fortunately, both groups valued honoring and obeying God over all else and were willing to reason together and come to an agreement. Acts 15:2 tells us the church in Antioch decided to send Paul and Barnabas to Jerusalem to see the apostles and elders, the recognized authorities of the Christian church at that time, to resolve the dilemma.

This gathering in Jerusalem included many if not all of the

remaining ten disciples who had walked with Jesus, some Pharisees who had become Christians, Paul, Barnabas, and James (Jesus's half brother, who was the acknowledged chair of the council). They first read the backstory by seeking to understand each other's perspectives. The Jerusalem Council, as it has become known to history, started with the Pharisees stating their case that Gentiles must be circumcised and follow the law of Moses (Acts 15:5). The apostle Peter then reminded them of his experiences in Caesarea, recorded in Acts 10, when the Roman centurion Cornelius and his friends and family received the Holy Spirit before they had an opportunity to be circumcised (Acts 15:7–11). Paul and Barnabas relayed their experiences sharing the gospel and planting churches among predominantly Gentile new Christians in what are now Cyprus and Turkey (v. 12). Everyone who had something to contribute spoke. Everyone listened and understood what the others believed and considered important. They all understood the reason for the conflict, and they were willing to ask how God might be at work.

They then sought to Catch God's Story. Although Luke records only James's words in the next section of the account, these words provide clear evidence of theological reflection. In verse 14, James pointed to the evidence of Peter's miraculous experience in Joppa. If the Army officer Cornelius and his Roman friends had received the Holy Spirit, how could anyone deny God's acceptance of them? Paul's and Barnabas's accounts of miracles also provided solid evidence of God's work among the uncircumcised. James next reflected on Scripture from the Prophet Amos and applied it to their situation. Most important of all, James noted that the Holy Spirit gave them guidance. He then made a clear decision in verse 19 not to require the Gentiles to be circumcised. But it was not just James's unilateral decision. Verses 22, 25, and 28 all use a particular Greek verb followed by a first person plural pronoun (us) to describe the decision's united nature. Verse 28 uses the wording, "It seemed good to the Holy Spirit and to us," verifying that God worked through the process to confirm what James decided and the Council agreed was the best answer to a question that had divided the church.

Since Catching God's Story made it clear that God did accept the Gentiles without circumcision, they were able to skip the steps of increasing and weighing options and move straight to developing a plan as they Crafted a New Story. They knew many churches had been brought into the debate and people were on both sides of the issue. There had to be a way to maintain unity within the young church. They chose to send a letter to churches around the world from the church's main leadership in Jerusalem, putting the letter in the hands of key leaders to circulate.

With this plan in place, it was time to Tell the New Story to churches, and how it was told mattered greatly. Paul, Barnabas, Barsabbas, and Silas delivered the letter. This team strategically blended those who had been leaders at Antioch and some who had been in Jerusalem in recent years. It showed unity where division had once ruled, and including respected leaders from a variety of perspectives ensured the widest acceptance possible. The wording of the letter itself was positive and clear. It was addressed from the apostles, those who had walked with Jesus, and the "elders," others with authority and respect, perhaps even some who had originally advocated for circumcision. It specifically communicated a clear, unified decision and the sense of the Holy Spirit's guidance in it. It also gave churches instructions for carrying out the decision (Acts 15:23–29).

The action they and the churches took led to a new season of health and growth in the Christian community and even greater unity. Paul returned to the churches to evaluate their acceptance and actions, and his letter to the Galatians likely corrected some lingering misunderstandings. Paul's visit to Jerusalem later, with an offering and representatives from many of the new Gentile churches, was likely a further Holy Spirit–inspired effort to continue the reconciliation and healing process.[3] Today, the church around the world still strongly communicates the message of God's love and grace because its early leaders were willing to shape its story in the right direction. This wonderful account of resolved corporate conflict provides a model for any organization or group seeking to chart a path forward in the midst of conflict. Let's look next at how we can use Story Shaping to work through relational conflict.

CHAPTER ELEVEN

GETTING STORIES STRAIGHT:
RESOLVING CONFLICT

Joe and Becca had been married for about six months when Becca first became concerned about Joe's spending. Everything else about their marriage had been wonderful. They were deeply in love while still being best friends. They enjoyed the same activities and food, and they found that healthy balance between time together and time alone that so few couples master. They shared the same faith and commitment to lifelong marriage. Everyone thought they were the perfect couple, but serious issues started to arise the day Becca decided to review the credit card bill.

They had agreed before the wedding that paying the bills would be Joe's responsibility. He had done better in math in high school, and Becca's dad had always paid the bills for their family. It seemed an appropriate responsibility for Joe to handle. So Becca was startled to find an outstanding Visa card balance of almost $4,000. They had opened the account on the plane on the way back from their honeymoon. Joe had convinced Becca that getting the card would be a good way to build up air miles so they could return to the Bahamas on their first anniversary. "We can use the card for our groceries and gasoline and other purchases,"

Joe said. "As long as we pay the balance off each month, we won't pay any interest, but we get credited one mile for every dollar we spend." Becca remembered what a huge celebration her parents had thrown the day they paid off their credit cards when she was in eighth grade. Her father had refused to allow her to get her own credit card because of all the problems he and her mother had in their marriage, but she hated to disappoint her new husband. Besides, the honeymoon was wonderful, and she would love to do it again every year.

The dismay of seeing such a large outstanding balance made her question her earlier agreement. When she saw Joe that evening, she asked him about it. "Joe, I saw the Visa statement in the trash. It says we have an outstanding balance of $4,000. Is that accurate?"

Joe immediately erupted in anger. "Why are you questioning me about that? We have had extra expenses lately. We needed to get some important things. I needed a lawn mower to take care of the yard. You wanted a new chair in the living room, right? I had to take a coworker out to dinner. Your birthday dinner last month was not exactly cheap. Neither was the gift. I was not going to go cheap on your first birthday with me as your husband. We'll get it paid off."

Becca felt immediate guilt for her doubt but also shock at Joe's reaction. She had never seen him get angry that way before. She hoped Joe was right, and they would pay off the balance soon, but it did not happen. A couple of months later, she picked up the mail and noticed an envelope in Joe's name that felt as though it had a credit card inside. She asked Joe about it when he came home. "It had a better interest rate than the airline card," he said curtly. Becca asked how they were progressing at paying the other bill. "We're working on it," was his quick reply. Yet Becca checked the next statement before Joe could open it and was upset to see it was maxed out at the $8,000 credit limit, mostly because of purchases at restaurants and stores she knew Joe liked. She was frightened and furious as she entered the second bedroom Joe had dubbed his "Man Cave" and saw all kinds of new sporting goods and electronic equipment. How would they ever be able to pay off the bills? Was this a sign of things to come? How could they survive?

Becca confronted Joe with the bill that night. He reacted with the loudest voice she had ever heard from him. "Why did you open the bill? I told you I would take care of it, and why did you enter my man cave? I can't believe you're accusing me of this. I need this stuff. If I am going to make it at work, I have to play golf with the guys. They always go out for lunch afterward, and I have to pay my share. Sometimes I have other lunch meetings, and the places these guys go are pricey. If I play the game right, I should be promoted next year. We can pay down the debt with the extra income, but it makes me angry that you don't trust me. Let me handle this!"

Becca gave in again. She was not used to anger. Her own father was even-tempered. In fact, he acquiesced to nearly all her mother's requests, so she had never experienced this kind of controlling behavior.

Their financial situation grew worse. Soon collectors were calling about unpaid bills. Becca tried to bring up the issue to find a solution, but Joe's anger erupted even more quickly and fiercely. "All you ever want to do is talk about money!" he would scream back at her. Becca was deeply afraid pressing the issue might lead to divorce, so she took a second job on her own to help pay down the debt. Joe responded by complaining that he never saw her anymore. Soon Becca found herself sandwiched between fear of bankruptcy and fear of Joe's anger and possible divorce. It felt as though she was on a plane about to crash.

Meanwhile, Joe had become more irritable about Becca's

obsession with their financial situation, and her need to control him was making him wonder whether he had done the wrong thing by marrying her. He did not believe in divorce, but this was not the happily ever after either of them had expected when they said, "I do." Neither Joe nor Becca could imagine their love returning.

In another city, Trudy and Tiffany had been very close while growing up. The sisters were two years apart and shared many happy memories of family vacations, playing dress-up in their mother's clothes and wrestling with Dad on the living room floor. Tiffany's marriage and career had taken her across the country, so both she and Trudy always looked forward to Thanksgivings together with their parents, until the year that their father died. Their mother had been in frail health and depended on him for nearly everything, so his heart attack caught them all by surprise. Since Trudy was closer, she offered to allow their mother, Eloise, to move in with her. But her Alzheimer's disease and physical ailments made taking care of her a full-time job. Trudy had a great career, and her family depended on both her and her husband's income. But her mother fought the idea of moving to a nursing home, so Trudy made the sacrifice to stop working. She rented out her parents' home to offset the income from her job, but it did not cover all the medical expenses. Trudy and her husband had to draw heavily from their children's college funds to stay afloat, and they canceled cherished family summer vacations to pay the bills. During all this, Tiffany rarely called, and Trudy barely had time to email her. Tiffany brought her family out the next Thanksgiving, but seeing her mother in such a frail state and not having her father there made the experience far more painful than pleasant. Soon Tiffany stopped calling and chose not to make the trip the next two Thanksgivings.

The third year after their father died, their mother, Eloise, suffered a brain aneurysm. Trudy called Tiffany from the hospital to let her know she would need to come quickly if she wanted to see their mother alive again. Tiffany agonized in emotional pain and wound up waiting two days before buying a plane ticket.

Tiffany arrived at the hospital just before Eloise passed away, but since Eloise was in a coma, Tiffany was not able to have a last conversation with her. This left her with a great deal of grief, since they had not spoken since that last Thanksgiving over two years earlier. Tiffany had only a week off work, so that meant Trudy not only had to plan the memorial service and reception alone but also had to ask Tiffany to make quick decisions about what heirlooms she would like to take with her. Trudy wanted to settle the estate quickly and get back to living a sustainable life.

They went to Eloise's room in Trudy's house the day before Tiffany was to leave. Sorting through Eloise's jewelry and pictures, Tiffany looked out the door and saw their mother's favorite rocking chair in the living room. "I will take her chair instead," she said.

Trudy was stunned. "What?" she exclaimed. "I wanted to keep it because she spent so many days in it during her last years here."

Tiffany had her own stunned reaction. "You got two years with her. I got nothing. I want that chair because it's the one she used to read to me in when I was a little girl."

Trudy became very angry. "I got two years? I actually had three years of no life aside from taking care of Mom. I had to give up my job, our vacations, my fun, and almost my husband, and you got . . . nothing? You were free to do whatever you wanted. You could have come here anytime you wanted, and you didn't even make it out for Thanksgivings. And now you want her chair, the one thing more than anything else that represents her to me!"

After tears and screams from both of them, Tiffany ran out the door, crying all the way to her hotel room.

STRAIGHTENING OUT DIFFERING STORIES

Conflict is a part of life. Since humanity's beginning, we have disagreed with one another, often at great cost. The fourth chapter of the Bible presents the first of many severe conflicts. This conflict cost Abel his life and Cain his social status. Unresolved conflicts have led to countless murders, wars, divorces, and suicides. Yet conflict does not have to stay unresolved. Story Shaping provides a model for resolving conflict in a healthy manner.

The same steps used for decision making apply: (1) Read the Backstory, (2) Catch God's Story, (3) Craft a New Story, and (4) Tell the New Story. A key difference, though, is considering whether you can or should work through the process with the person with whom you are having the conflict. You have three choices. The first is to walk through the process with the other party. This option is best if the other party is willing. Jesus was clear that if we are aware that a brother or sister has something against us, we are to go to that person and be reconciled (Matthew 5:23–24). If we have something against someone else, we should also take the initiative and go to them (Matthew 18:15). Either way, we ought to take initiative to resolve conflict whether we started it or someone else did.

However, in some instances a second option may be better, that of walking through the process on our own, then walking through it with the other. Conflicts are emotional, and many of us do not think rationally when upset. Taking time to sort our thoughts can help us to use better reasoning when we do seek to reconcile. But we must remain humble and willing to listen. Any conclusions we reach on our own should be tentative and open for reconsideration after we hear the other person's perspective. The third option, walking through the process on our own, should be used only when the other party is not willing to reconcile.

Romans 12:18 says, "If it is possible, as far as it depends on you, live at peace with everyone."

In other words, it is not always possible to live at peace with everyone. You can still work through the process to determine your best response. Sometimes your actions may lead to change in the other person. Proverbs 25:21–22 describes such an occurrence: "If your enemy is hungry, give him food to eat; if he is thirsty, give him water to drink. In doing this, you will heap burning coals on his head, and the LORD will reward you." Intentional, wise action on your part may eventually lead to reconciliation even if the person is not initially willing to try to resolve the issue.

1. Read the Other's Backstory

Once you have decided that you will work through the process with the other party, it is time to begin. Reading the Backstory includes determining the source and nature of the conflict. Sometimes people have a severe argument, but each party thinks it is over something different. Suppose a friend offered to pick you up from the garage when you took your car in for service, but did not show up. Later you run into a coworker who said he enjoyed a fun round of golf with your friend that afternoon. You fumed with anger because your friend chose to play golf with your coworker rather than keep a commitment to you. You may have assumed your friend did not keep his word because he lacks integrity. This leads you to cut off the relationship with your friend, and you let him know. Your friend is shocked, hurt, and confused by the relational break. He decides not to pick you up *next week* from the mechanic's shop, the appointment you told him about. You had given your friend the wrong date!

Start by writing down the specific disagreement. Then identify the factors that contributed to it. Why is there a disagreement? Be sure to include a discussion of the lens layers you each hold. Conflict is often a result of differences in one or more lens layers, intentional or intuitive, between the parties involved.

In our first story, Becca held the belief that not paying credit cards off regularly would lead to increasing and out-of-control debt. Her birth family's experience embedded an ethic that debt was bad. She also inherited an ethic that family conflicts and anger were bad. The conflict with her husband over the debt put these two ethics, to have no debt and to not make her spouse angry, in opposition to each other. The circumstances also challenged Becca's values of serenity and sustainability. She reasoned that approaching Joe for clarification would enable them to find a solution. But Joe's anger every time left her with a strong intuitive desire to avoid the conflict altogether. Although she hoped things would get better, the reality of the situation soon led her to reason that things could not improve without a change.

Joe's lenses differed from Becca's. He believed God would provide for them. Is that not what Matthew 6:33 promises? Joe also sincerely believed he would be promoted if he regularly hobnobbed with the corporate executives. He was succeeding at his job, and Joe's supervisors appreciated him. He held an ethic that it was not right for a wife to confront a husband over something like spending. He was the man and the primary breadwinner and bill payer in their family, so his ethic said his wife should not question his spending decisions. He also believed such questions were rooted in contempt. How could their marriage be healthy if his wife did not respect him? The values of recreation and social connection were much higher on his list than savings and privation. Joe also did not make an effort to reason and consider the outcomes of his choices or to acknowledge how surrendering to his intuitive desires had increased their debt and Becca's fears.

Conflict is usually best resolved by listening before speaking. Do not assume you know the other person's beliefs, ethics, values, and reasoning. Ask questions to help you understand. Most people hold their beliefs, ethics, and values so deeply they do not recognize them as lens layers that others may not share. Many assume others hold the same beliefs, ethics, and values. A young husband may believe "cleanliness is next to godliness" and that it is ethically wrong not to keep a house clean. Yet his wife values relaxed conversation on the couch more than a spotless floor. He gets mad at her clutter, and she gets hurt by the lack of time together. Unless they work to find out what each person believes, values, and holds as right, wrong, good, and bad, the hard feelings will multiply over time and resentment will undermine what could be a healthy marriage.

Here are some questions you can consider about the lens layers at play in a conflict:

- Belief lens
  - What created this dilemma?
  - What factors are at work?
  - How did I contribute to the problem?
  - How did others contribute?
  - What happens if we do nothing?
- Ethics lens
  - What is right or wrong about this situation?
  - What is good or bad and better or worse?
  - Where did I get my ethics about this?
- Values lens
  - What matters most in this conflict?
  - What is worth losing to gain the most important item at risk?
  - What would the others say they value most?
- Reason lens
  - Why do we disagree?
  - How can we best resolve this?

- Impulses lens
  - What habits have contributed to this problem?
  - Is one of us seeking to fulfill a desire that is opposed to one of our ethics or values?

2. God's Story Is Reconciliation

Once we have identified what is happening in our disagreement and why it is happening, we now want to catch God's story. As we have already seen, God ultimately desires reconciliation. He values it so much he sent his only Son to reconcile us to himself (2 Corinthians 5:19–20). The Bible urges us to suffer personal loss if it can lead to the restoration of a relationship (Matthew 5:38–42; 1 Corinthians 6:7). Sometimes, like Christ, we need to stand against injustice and be willing to refute those who lead from false motives and teach in error (Matthew 23 and Titus 1:9–11). Do not compromise truth, but never stop seeking to restore relationship. Walking through the often painful process of reconciliation catches the heart of God's story.

3. Crafting a New Story

Step 3, Crafting a New Story, usually involves seeking a mutually agreeable outcome. The same process for decision making works well:

1. Increase the number of options.
2. Reduce the options to a manageable number.
3. Evaluate the remaining options.
4. Make a decision.[1]

The key component is increasing ideas to break away from the narrow framing that often arises in highly emotional settings. We tend to default to a "your way or my way" thought process.

In such a context, one person wins and the other loses. Yet the best solution is often not one of the two starting options. Taking time to expand options first may introduce a better solution. Even if you eventually decide on one of the initial positions, the intensity of the disagreement may subside by listening to each other as you take time to consider all options.

Writing down ideas as you increase options can help you keep track of them and remind you that the disagreement, not the other person, is the enemy. Let the ideas flow without judgment or criticism until you feel you have written down as many as you can. I suggest considering the following approaches as options during a disagreement.

- *Acknowledge a misunderstanding.* As mentioned earlier, many disagreements are simply misunderstandings. Once you sit down together and read the backstory, you may find that forgiving one another is all that is required to restore the relationship and move forward.

- *One yields to the other.* In this case, one party yields to the request of the other. This is often the quickest way to resolve a conflict, but it is not always the best. Some families, like Becca's, train children with an ethic that says all disagreement is bad. A child from such a home may yield in every conflict, even when the action of the other party is harmful for everyone involved. But there are other occasions when it is best if a person simply acknowledges their fault and seeks forgiveness. An excellent biblical example is King David's repentance after the Prophet Nathan confronted him for his adultery and murder plot (2 Samuel 11–12).

- *Compromise.* People in disagreements can choose to meet in the middle. Both sides may give up something to appease the other and restore the relationship. Sometimes this is advisable because it can be quick and fair. However, usually neither side gets what they want in a compromise. Quite often there is a better decision.

- *Find a win-win.* One of Stephen Covey's very influential *Seven Habits of Highly Effective People* is "Think Win/Win."[2] In a disagreement, both parties may find a way to come out of it with what they truly value. Such a resolution is ideal in any conflict. But it is not always simple to find the win/win. The next item can help.

- *Find another solution.* Increasing options beyond what both parties brought to the disagreement makes this possible. Brainstorming and lateral thinking can help grow the list as large as possible.

- *Bring in a mediator.* When parties in conflict cannot reach a mutually acceptable agreement, it can be wise to bring in a third party that does not take either side but works for reconciliation. This was the apostle Paul's suggestion for the Corinthian church. They had been taking their conflicts to secular courts. Paul abhorred this option and pleaded for them to have a wise believer among them settle their disputes (1 Corinthians 6:5). Similarly, in Philippians 4:2–3, Paul urged a "true companion" to help Euodia and Syntyche resolve their disagreement. A mediator can reduce personal attacks, keep discussion focused on the real problem, and increase the likelihood of finding a mutually acceptable outcome.

Once your list of options is as large as is reasonably possible, work through the list, eliminating any that are disagreeable to both of you. We naturally want to keep our favorite ideas, but seek to remain as open as possible during the elimination until a few

good options are left. These options can now be thoroughly evaluated and discussed. It is best if both parties are willing to consider
a different future than they had envisioned. Identifying deeply
held values can aid both sides in understanding what matters most
to the other. Seek a way to achieve as much as possible for both
parties, then make a decision. It may be best to make the decision
tentative and allow time to test it, especially when it deals with a
recurring issue.

The final part of Crafting a New Story is developing the plan
to implement it. Depending on the nature of the conflict, the
plan may include an extensive and detailed list of activities for all
involved, or it may require a single action. Be sure to assign the
appropriate person for each step and include a specific time for
follow-up and evaluation.

4. Telling the New Story

The final step, Tell the New Story, is important when
the conflict has affected others. Those directly involved in the
conflict may have shared their side of the story with friends. This
often creates factions. Unless the parties notify everyone involved
of their resolution, the factions will remain, and relationships can
be poisoned. Make a list of all the people impacted by the conflict
and determine who will discuss the outcome with them. How
both sides tell the story is important. Do not paint the other side
as evil or wrong. Do not gloat in a "victory." Instead, let people
know the issue has been resolved. Taking the actions agreed upon
is critical, and evaluating the decision at the agreed upon times
can lead to further improvements in the situation and the renewed
relationship.

Becca knew her family's finances would not improve unless
she took action. It would not be easy. She loved Joe and was committed to a life of love together, but it would take real change to

make their marriage last. She prayed hard, got courageous, walked through the Story-Shaping process on her own, then asked Joe for a meeting to come up with a mutually agreeable solution.

Joe anticipated what was coming. He hated the conversations about money and resented his wife's implications, but he had to admit there was a problem. When she asked for an hour at the kitchen table on Thursday evening, he agreed.

Becca started out positively. "Joe, thanks so much for taking time to discuss this. Talking about finances has been hard for both of us. I deeply love you, and I am fully committed to spending the rest of my life with you. I know you are committed too, right?" Joe nodded, and Becca continued, "I want our marriage to be the best it can possibly be, and that means we have to be willing and able to work through disagreements like this. My goal is not to get you to agree with me tonight. My goal is for us to find something on which we can both agree that is sustainable for the long term. I know God wants that for us too, so let's pray and ask him to help us. In fact, you can pray if you would like."

Joe was taken aback by that offer but agreed and prayed that God would give them wisdom, unity, and long-term success. Becca explained the Story-Shaping approach to finding a solution that both felt was a win. She pointed out the first thing they needed to do was identify the specific dilemma and write it down. "I'd like for us find a way to live within our income that is agreeable to both of us. Does that sound okay to you?"

Joe replied, "If you mean that we do not go further into debt except in urgent circumstances, yes, I am okay with that as the issue to resolve."

Becca hesitated, "We may need to qualify what those urgent circumstances might be, but this can at least get us started." She wrote down on a piece of paper, "How will we live within our means and not increase our debt except in urgent circumstances?"

Becca then explained her own intentional lens, including the belief that if they continued to spend more than they made, they could go bankrupt, lose their house, and undermine future opportunities. She also explained the conflicted ethical layer of her lens, where she needed to make her husband happy while also viewing unsecured debt as bad and wrong. She asked Joe whether she understood him correctly. "It seems to me you believe God will provide for us no matter what we do, so we should not be worried about borrowing too much. Is that true?"

"Well, I would not put it that way," Joe replied. "I just think we should not worry about it too much. In addition, I really do believe I might be promoted next year, but you are right. Borrowing too much is not wise."

"Thanks for saying that, Joe. Do I read your ethics correctly? Do you think it is wrong for me, as your wife, to confront you?"

"Again, I would not use those words," Joe replied. "The Bible says for a wife to respect her husband. When you treat me with contempt, it makes me angry. But we do have to be able to work things out. I appreciate the attitude you are showing tonight. It helps that you are taking the time to listen to me."

"I always want to listen to you, Joe. We need to both win with what we decide. I think there may be one more ethic you hold. Do you feel there is a certain minimum lifestyle that is acceptable for us?"

"I never thought of it that way, but I guess I do feel like I should be able to go golfing and eat out at least once a week. Is that what you mean?"

"Yes," Becca replied. "I think part of this conflict stems from me wanting to do without some things now if it means we can be financially stable for the long term. I saw how hard it was for my parents when they had crushing debt in my elementary years. I also saw how much it freed them to pay it all off by the time I turned fourteen. My dad pounded the value of debt-free living into us. I appreciate the good life, though, and I know how much it means to you. That's why I want to find a way that works for us."

"Me too," said Joe. "What's next?"

"We Catch God's Story," Becca replied. She pulled out several prepared Bible verses that talk about the importance of paying what is owed (Romans 13:7–8; 2 Thessalonians 3:8) and the risk of borrowing (Proverbs 22:7), but she also pointed out passages on God's provision (Matthew 6:33; 2 Corinthians 9:8). She even included Ephesians 5:22, "Wives submit yourselves to your own husbands as you do to the Lord."

"I like that one," Joe said, "but I know what comes next, 'Husbands, love your wives, just as Christ loved the church.' That is a tall order. It is clear that we need to pay off our debts, but also that God provides."

Becca agreed and asked whether either of them sensed a leading from the Holy Spirit yet. "I had a deep conviction to get this resolved. That could be from God. I also have hope we can find a mutually agreeable solution. Do you sense anything specific from God?"

Joe said, "I am not sure yet. I certainly want to be open to what he wants us to do."

"Indeed!" Becca agreed. "But since we do not have clear direction for a course of action yet, let's see how many ideas we can come up with."

"You can work full time at a better paying job," Joe suggested.

Becca resented this because she felt she was already doing as much as she could, but she knew if she reacted negatively to Joe's ideas, he would shut down hers, so she said, "Okay," and wrote it down on the page. "What else?"

"I can ask for a raise," Joe said, "I doubt I will get one yet, and it might hurt me if I seem entitled."

"We can at least write it down," replied Becca. "We do not want to stop the ideas flowing. We could sell the house and rent a smaller apartment."

"No! I do not want to rent. We lose equity, and we have to put up with someone else's problems," Joe rebuffed.

"It is just an idea," replied Becca. "Let's keep it on the list for now. Remember, no criticism up front. We can pull off all bad ideas once we complete the list. What about getting some help?"

"Do you mean a financial counselor?"

"Sure . . . or at least maybe. We could sign up for the Financial Peace University course at church."

"Those are both ideas we can put down. What about borrowing from my parents to pay off the credit cards and developing a long-term payment plan with them?"

"I'm not sure I like that," Becca replied, "but it is an idea, so it goes on the list. Do you realize we have not even put down 'develop and live by a budget'?"

"I'm sure that would be part of FPU or counseling, but we could probably do it on our own with Quicken or one of those apps. Put it on the list."

Joe and Becca threw out some other ideas, but eventually they felt the list was complete enough to begin to reduce it. Becca explained to Joe what that meant, but Joe replied, "Becca, some of these steps could go together. For example, until we create a budget, we will not know whether we make enough money to pay our bills and debts in our current arrangement. If it works, you would not need to work full time, and we would not need to consider selling the house."

"That is true," Becca replied. "Perhaps the best first step is to do a budget, but are we better to do that on our own, with a counselor, or with Financial Peace University?"

"Well, I know how to create a budget," Joe answered. "I do

not really want other people knowing about our finances. I would rather we did this together first."

"I'm okay with that as long as you keep informed about how we are really doing and we can come up with a way to be sure our debt does not increase."

"We are a team, aren't we?" Joe smiled. "I will get all our expenses together and make a chart that shows how much we need to spend on bills, how much we have left for food, entertainment, and other items, and then compare that to our income."

"How can we be sure we do not spend more than we decide?" Becca interjected.

"There is an app for that!" Joe smiled. "If we give each other access, it will track our spending."

"You will really be okay with me knowing how much you spend and where?"

"As long as you are respectful when you point it out, I think it will be fine. We can test it for a month or two and see if it works. If we are getting all our bills paid and have some money in savings, and we are both comfortable with the arrangement, I think it will be fine."

"I agree," Becca replied. "I like that solution. We can even set a date for two months from tonight to follow up and see if things are going well. So the plan is that you will get the expenses and income chart together, we will discuss the amounts for each item, we will use the app to track our spending and hold each other accountable, and then we will meet again in two months to see if this solution is working."

"That's it!" Joe exclaimed. "This is not nearly as bad as I expected."

Joe and Becca told the new story by taking the actions they had agreed upon and following up in two months. They needed to adjust some of their budgeted amounts in different categories, but it seemed to be a win for both of them.

Trudy and Tiffany's situation was quite a bit different. As sisters rather than spouses, the dynamics of their relationship were different. They did not see each other every day, and their actions did not usually affect each other. But the loss of their mother and father affected them both deeply. Tiffany's request for her mother's rocking chair angered Trudy, but she understood they needed to resolve the argument. Their long-term emotional health required them to be able to move forward while still having some connection with each other and the memories of their parents. Trudy decided to take action for reconciliation. She called Tiffany and asked whether they could meet at a coffee shop to get things resolved before Tiffany went home. Tiffany agreed.

"Tiffany, I know losing Mom has hurt us both deeply. I do not understand a lot about your actions the past few years. That is why I was shocked when you asked for the chair. But I do not want you to go back home with this hanging over us. We both need to heal. I am not sure that can happen if we are angry and divided. I read a book called *How to Make Big Decisions Wisely* that lays out a process for reconciling disagreements. Is it okay if I explain it? You can then decide if you would like to try to use it to make a decision on the rocking chair."

Tiffany agreed, and Trudy explained how the process works. They identified "decide on the chair" as the issue to resolve.

Trudy realized their lenses were likely a significant part of the conflict. Trudy held an ethic of responsibility. In her mind, Tiffany had violated that by her absence, not only in not caring for their mother but also in not communicating. She did not believe it was right or fair for Tiffany to get the chair. Although this was a strong conviction for her, she was afraid that saying it first might shut down the conversation, so instead she focused on understanding Tiffany's lenses. "Tiffany, you said you believe you should have Mom's rocker to be able to remember her from your childhood, right? You also said you felt that way especially because you did not get to see her these last few years. Can you tell me your reasoning for not visiting her and why you believe it is more right for you to have the chair than me?"

Tiffany was not sure she could share everything. She was hurt by the loss of their mother. She was also hurt by Trudy's reaction when she said she would take the chair instead of the jewelry they had been going through. Growing up, she had never seen Trudy so angry. Trudy's attack hurt, but it only hardened Tiffany's resolve to hold out for the chair, even though she agreed about wanting to restore their relationship. The coming years would be hard enough to face without her sister. She wasn't sure why the chair was so important to her. She tried to put her thoughts and feelings together in a way that made sense.

"Trudy, there were a lot of reasons I didn't visit. For one, it is expensive to fly across the country. Neither Bob nor I have had a pay raise in years, but our expenses have continued to increase. And there is more to it. That Thanksgiving three years ago was difficult. It was not the same without Dad, and seeing Mom suffering so much hurt me too. It was weird having it at your house. I know we had no other choice, and you were a great host. I just could not stand to be there with all that emotion. It was not an ethical thing. It even violated my values, as you call them, of family and togetherness to not be there the next year. In fact, I think the value of togetherness being broken is what hurt so much. It hurt every day. It even hurts now. I'm sorry. I can't undo what I've done. I am so sorry."

Trudy then realized what had seemed an intentional, reasoned decision to cut off the relationship and dump all the work and responsibility on her was really an intuitive (but impulsive) reaction on Tiffany's part to the deep pain she had felt. Trudy could have forgiven her right then, but she wanted Tiffany to understand what she had experienced. She explained about the expenses, the loss of the job and vacations, the emotional grief at watching their mother suffer, and the inability to explain to their mother why Tiffany never called. Soon both were crying.

"I'm so, so sorry!" Tiffany cried out more than once.

Catching God's story at that point was unmistakable. The Lord's Prayer asks God to forgive us as we forgive our brothers and sisters. Trudy knew she had to forgive. Other Bible passages quickly came to her mind too, including one from Luke 6: "Give to everyone who asks you." Trudy decided to offer the chair to her sister.

"No, you don't have to do that," Tiffany responded.

"It's okay," Trudy replied. "I know now why you weren't here. I want you to have something to remember her."

Although the sisters could have walked through the process of brainstorming options, Trudy kept insisting until Tiffany accepted. She had many more things to help her remember those last few years with their mother. Just learning that what had seemed to be selfish disinterest on Tiffany's part was in fact an unintentional emotion-driven reaction to great pain enabled Trudy to want Tiffany to take the chair. A restored relationship with her sister was worth more than a chair.

CHAPTER **TWELVE**

EPILOGUE:
WHAT'S YOUR STORY?

Your life is a story, and your story is part of a much larger story, woven together by the Greatest Storyteller of all time. Believing in Jesus and putting him first is the best decision any of us can make and the key to living the best story possible. As Proverbs 9:10–12 says, "The fear of the LORD is the beginning of wisdom, and knowledge of the Holy One is understanding. For through wisdom your days will be many, and years will be added to your life. If you are wise, your wisdom will reward you." Once we trust in Christ, commit to living his way, and pursue his wisdom, we are ready to begin shaping our stories well when we face big decisions.

Yet as we venture through our stories, we do not always make wise decisions. Perhaps reading this book has brought to mind times you could have used these principles but didn't. Rather than intentionally seeking God's story or crafting a good story, you made an impulsive decision that ended a once-cherished relationship, killed a promising career, or brought a physical torment that changed the course of your life.

There are some things we can't undo, and we can't convince everyone to like us and forgive us. But the best news ever is that

God will. First John 1:9 says, "If we confess our sins, he is faithful and just and will forgive us our sins and purify us from all unrighteousness." This wonderful promise means that even when we mess up our story, God is eager to rewrite it for us and provide a powerful plot twist that brings a happier ending than we could have ever imagined.

We don't need to live in guilt. When we receive the gift of God's grace by faith in Jesus Christ, we are forgiven. We are a new creation. The past is over, and an incredible new future awaits.

The first step of Story Shaping, Reading the Backstory, is important because we can learn from our mistakes and successes, and we can come to a better understanding of the current situation and what led to it. But we should not dwell on the past any longer than necessary.

Look at your front windshield the next time you get into your car, then look at your rearview mirror. That mirror is important. It will help you drive more safely. It can warn you that a car is coming up on your left side before you change lanes. That mirror may save your life sometime. But look at what a small percentage of your windshield is taken up by that rearview mirror. A good driver's eyes are on the road ahead far more than in the mirror looking backward. Live your life that way. Spend more time and energy crafting your new stories than living in regret over your backstories.

How you choose to shape your story today will affect more than just your future. Every decision you make will affect others. Every conversation you have may change another's story. Intentionally shaping your story every day to catch God's story, craft a new story, and then tell it and live it out will change the world.

Remember, your story is part of the great never-ending story. Even as our decisions shape our lives and influence those around us, God is at work. The apostle Paul strove to describe the indescribable eternal story by citing Isaiah 64:4: "'What no eye has seen, what no ear has heard, and what no human mind has conceived'—the things God has prepared for those who love him" (1 Corinthians 2:9). C. S. Lewis beautifully and memorably articulated God's story at the end of *The Last Battle*, wrapping up his wonderful *Chronicles of Narnia* series.

> And for us this is the end of all of the stories, and we can truly say that they all lived happily ever after. But for them it was only the beginning of the real story. All their life in this world and all the adventures in Narnia had only been the cover and the title page: now at last they were beginning Chapter One of the Great Story which no one on earth has ever read: which goes on forever: in which every chapter is better than the one before.[1]

The Great Story that awaits us is beyond anything we can imagine. It starts now. How we choose to live our stories will affect not only how we experience that Great Story but also how those we lead and love will. What will you do? Will you let your story just happen? I hope instead you will make decisions to live your story well, letting your story shape others' stories as we live out God's story together.

NOTES

Chapter 1: The Challenge and Opportunity of Big Decisions

1. Jerome Cottin, "The Evolution of Practical Theology in French Speaking Europe," *International Journal of Practical Theology* 17, no.1 (2013): 33.

Chapter 2: When Quick Decisions Are Best

1. Daniel Kahneman, *Thinking, Fast and Slow* (New York: Farrar, Straus & Giroux, 2011).

2. Some term this theory the Heuristic Systems Method, including Richard E. Petty, Pablo Brinol, and Zakary L. Tormala, "Thought Confidence as a Determinant of Persuasion: The Self-Validation Hypothesis," *Journal of Personality and Social Psychology* 82, no. 5 (2002): 722–41; James B. Stiff and Paul A. Mongeau, *Persuasive Communication* (New York: Guilford, 2003), 233; and Duane T. Wegener and Richard E. Petty, "Understanding the Effects of Mood through the Elaboration Likelihood and Flexible Correction Models," in Leonard L. Martin and Gerald L. Clare, *Theories of Mood and Cognition: A User's Guide* (Mahwah, NJ: Erlbaum, 2001), 177–210. Others use the title Elaboration Likelihood Method, in Richard M. Perloff, *The Dynamics of Persuasion: Communication and Attitudes in the 21st Century* (Mahwah, NJ: Erlbaum, 2003), 128–42; and Stiff and Mongeau, *Persuasive Communication*, 217–35.

3. The concept of heuristics as a means of quick decision making was developed by Allen Newell and Herbert A. Simon, *Human Problem Solving* (Englewood Cliffs, NJ: Prentice Hall, 1972).

4. Jonah Berger, *Invisible Influence: The Hidden Forces that Shape Behavior* (New York: Simon & Schuster, 2016), 196. Berger's sources are Robert Zajonc, A. Heingart, and E. Herman, "Social Enhancement and Impairment of Performance in the Cockroach," *Journal of Personality and Social Psychology* 13 (1969): 83; Hazel Markus, "The Effect of Mere Presence on Social Facilitation: An Unobtrusive Test," *Journal of Experimental Psychology* 14 (1978): 389–97; and J. W. Michaels, J. M. Blommel, R. M. Brocato, R. A. Linkous, and J. S. Rowe, "Social Facilitation and Inhibition in a Natural Setting," *Replications in Social Psychology* 2 (1982): 21–14.

5. William James, *Principles of Psychology, vol. 2* (New York: Dover, 1952), 389.

6. John Kounlos and Mark Beeman, *The Eureka Factor: Aha Moments, Creative Insight, and the Brain* (New York: Random House, 2015), 53–54.

7. David DiSalvo, *Brain Changer: How Harnessing Your Brain's Power to Adapt Can Change Your Life* (Dallas: BenBella, 2013), 70.

8. Jonah Lehrer, *How We Decide* (New York: Houghton-Mifflin, 2009).

9. In case you are still wondering, the ball cost five cents, and the bat cost $1.05.

10. Kahneman, *Thinking*, 44.

11. Daniel Goleman, *Working with Emotional Intelligence* (New York: Bantam, 1998), 74–76.

12. Jonathan Haidt first introduced this metaphor in *The Happiness Hypothesis* (New York: Basic Books, 2006). He developed the concept further in *The Coddling of the American Mind*, written with Greg Lukianoff (New York: Penguin, 2018), to describe what they see as one of the core good intentioned "bad ideas" that are setting America up for failure.

13. J. S. B. T. Evans, "Spot the Difference: Distinguishing Between Two Kinds of Processing," *Mind & Society*, 11, no. 1 (2012): 121–31. Kahneman, *Thinking*, 31–49, also provides much

evidence for how much energy the brain consumes in the System 1 (intentional) process.

14. Malcolm Gladwell, *Outliers: The Story of Success* (New York: Little, Brown, 2008), 35–68, and Daniel Coyle, *The Talent Code: Greatness Isn't Born. It's Grown. Here's How* (New York: Bantam, 2009), 9–94.

15. Emily P. Freeman, *The Next Right Thing: A Simple, Soulful Practice for Making Life Decisions* (Grand Rapids: Revell, 2019).

Chapter 3: How the Apostle Paul Decided

1. Carl Henry, *God, Revelation, and Authority, Volume II: God Who Speaks and Shows* (Waco: Word, 1976), 14–15.

2. Garry Friesen and J. Robin Maxson, *Decision Making and the Will of God: A Biblical Alternative to the Traditional View* (Portland, OR: Multnomah, 1980), 82.

3. Kevin DeYoung, *Taking God at His Word: Why the Bible Is Knowable, Necessary, and Enough and What That Means for You and Me* (Wheaton, IL: Crossway, 2014), 44.

4. Kevin DeYoung, *Just Do Something: A Liberating Approach to Finding God's Will* (Chicago: Moody Publishers, 2009), front cover.

5. DeYoung, *Just Do Something*, 24.

6. Paul Tillich, *Systematic Theology, Volume I: Reason and Revelation, Being, and God* (Chicago: University of Chicago Press, 1951), 127–32.

7. H. Richard Niebuhr, *The Meaning of Revelation* (New York: Macmillan, 1946), 136.

8. Dallas Willard, *Hearing God* (Downers Grove, IL: IVP, 2012), 120.

9. Karl Barth, *Church Dogmatics, Volume I:1, The Doctrine of the Word of God* (Edinburgh: T&T Clark, 1960), 518–19.

10. Karl Barth, *Church Dogmatics, Volume I:2, The Outpouring of the Holy Spirit* (Edinburgh: T&T Clark, 1960), 223.

11. Stanley Frodsham, *Spirit Filled, Led, and Taught* (Springfield, MO: Gospel Publishing, 1952), 33.

12. I had completed the draft for this book when I participated in the 2018 Society of Biblical Literature Annual Meeting in Denver, Colorado. On November 19, 2018, Mark Wilson presented a

paper there entitled "Odegoology and the Will of God: Is the Book of Acts 'Normative' for Divine Guidance?" that makes a case similar to this chapter's that the pattern of special revelation Paul received in Acts can serve as a standard for Christians today. Wilson's *The Spirit Said Go: Lessons in Guidance from Paul's Journeys* (Eugene, OR: Wipf & Stock, 2017) draws twenty "lessons" on the variety of ways God led Paul in Acts with current-day illustrations from his own life and the experiences of a variety of other Christian leaders and thinkers.

13. Acts 13:1–2 (This passage says the Holy Spirit commissioned Paul and Barnabas on their first journey. Although it does not explicitly state how this happened, the fact that 13:1 mentions prophets in the church at Antioch implies this is how the Holy Spirit spoke.); 1 Timothy 4:14.

14. Acts 9:12; 16:9; 18:9–10; 23:11; 27:23–25; 2 Corinthians 12:1–4; Galatians 1:12; 2:1–2.

15. Acts 11:29; 15:22; 19:21; 20:3, 16; 2 Corinthians 9:7.

16. For a few examples, see Acts 9:23–25, 29–30; 11:25–26; 13:42, 45–51; 14:5–6; 15:37–40; 16:13, 15, 18, 39; 17:2, 10, 14; 20:13, 16; 21:1, 13; 23:6, 16–18; 26:9.

17. Romans 1:10 and 15:32; 1 Corinthians 4:19 and 16:7; Hebrews 6:3; 1 Peter 3:17; and James 4:15.

18. Acts 26:17–18. In this passage, Paul is retelling his Damascus Road encounter in greater detail than in its first recording in chapter 9.

19. For example, the vision of the Macedonian man in Acts 16:9 led Paul to shift continents, the vision of Jesus in Acts 18:9–10 led Paul to stay longer in Corinth (and, later, Ephesus) rather than leaving when opposition arose, an apparently internal voice of the Holy Spirit directed Paul to take a relief offering to Jerusalem (see Acts 19:21; 20:1–4; 21:10; 1 Corinthians 16:1–4; 2 Corinthians 8:1–15, 19; 9:1–14; Romans 15:26–29), and in Acts 23:11 Jesus visited him with the promise he would testify in Rome as a prisoner.

20. Acts 11:27–28; 13:1–2, 9–12; 14:9–10; 15:28; 16:9–10; 21:11; 27:23–26; 1 Corinthians 14:26–33; 1 Timothy 4:14.

Chapter 4: Our Story-Reading Glasses

1. Kenneth Archer, "Pentecostal Hermeneutics and the Society for Pentecostal Studies," *Pneuma 37* (2015): 327–28.

2. Practical theology acknowledges that humans interpret everything they experience. Because of this, many writers have sought to understand how people interpret things and how that relates to our understanding of how God is at work in the world and what our role is as individuals to understand him, his purpose for us, and how we interact with others. The following sources go into greater detail on the work of interpretation (also called hermeneutics): Sally A. Brown, "Hermeneutics in Protestant Practical Theology," *Opening the Field of Practical Theology: An Introduction*, Kathleen Cahalan and Gordon S. Mikosi, eds. (Lanham, MD: Rowman and Littlefield, 2014); Elaine Graham, *Transforming Practice: Pastoral Theology in an Age of Uncertainty* (Eugene, OR: Wipf & Stock, 2002); Charles V. Gerkin, *The Living Human Document: Revision Pastoral Counseling in a Hermeneutical Mode* (Nashville, TN: Abingdon, 1984); Stanley Hauerwas, *The Peaceable Kingdom: A Primer in Christian Ethics* (Notre Dame, IN: Notre Dame University Press, 1983); and Richard Osmer, *Practical Theology: An Introduction*, (Grand Rapids: Eerdmans, 2008), 21–23.

3. Dale M. Coulter, "On Traditions, Local Traditions, and Discernment," *Pneuma 36* (2014): 1–3, identifies that early Christian tradition developed as a common identity that sought to integrate orthodoxy, orthopraxis, and orthopathy: right beliefs, right practice (ethics), and right values. These correspond to the intentional story lens.

4. Carol Dweck, *Mindset: The New Psychology of Success* (New York: Random House, 2006).

5. Shannon Chamberlain, "Adam Smith and the Romance Novel," *The Atlantic* (September 3, 2014).

6. Jerel P. Calzo and Monique Ward, "Media Exposure and Viewers' Attitudes Toward Homosexuality: Evidence for Mainstreaming or Resonance?" *Journal of Broadcasting & Electronic Media* (2009): 280–99; David Gauntlett, *Media, Gender, and Identity: An Introduction* (New York: Routledge, 2008); Jennifer M.

Bonds-Raacke, Elizabeth T. Cady, Rebecca Schlegel, Richard
J. Harris, and Lindsey Firebaugh, "Remembering Gay/Lesbian
Media Characters," *Journal of Homosexuality* 53, no. 3 (2007):
19–34.

7. Don Beck and Christopher Cowan, *Spiral Dynamics: Mastering
Values, Leadership, and Change* (New York: Blackwell Business,
1996).

8. Soren Kierkegaard, *Journals and Papers, vol. 5* (Bloomington, IN:
Indiana University Press, 1978), 5.

9. Kahneman, *Thinking*, 178.

10. Matthew B. Crawford, *The World Beyond Your Head: On
Becoming an Individual in an Age of Distraction* (New York:
Farrar, Strauss & Giroux, 2015), 33.

11. Daniel Coyle, *The Talent Code* (New York: Bantam, 2009), 33–50.

12. Frank Partnoy, *Wait: The Art and Science of Delay* (Philadelphia:
Perseus Books Group, 2012), 63–80.

13. Charles Duhigg, *The Power of Habit* (New York: Random House,
2012), 17.

14. Duhigg, *Habit*, 19.

15. In addition to several examples in Duhigg, Michael Moss, *Sugar
Salt Fat: How the Food Giants Hooked Us* (New York: Random
House, 2013), details specific scientific research efforts conducted
by food processing companies to make food as addictive as possible.

Chapter 5: Step 1: Read the Backstory

1. Mark Lasswell, "Lost in Translation," *CNN Money*, August 1,
2004.

2. Story Shaping is a practice-theory-practice approach to problem
solving and strategic change that starts with Reading the
Backstory. Many other approaches to change, especially business
models and other planning approaches, including church strategic
planning methods, such as that developed by Aubrey Malphurs,
Advanced Strategic Planning, Third Edition (Grand Rapids:
Baker, 2013), 91–144, and Alton Garrison, *A Spirit Empowered
Church: An Acts 2 Ministry Model* (Springfield, MO: Influence
Resources, 2015), begin with theory, then work toward practice.

The practice-theory-practice approach was codified by practical theology pioneers such as Don S. Browning, *A Fundamental Practical Theology* (Minneapolis: Fortress, 1991), 285.

3. David Cooperrider and Suresh Srivastva, "Appreciative Inquiry into Organizational Life," *Research in Organizational Change and Development*, vol 1, W. A. Pasmore and R. W. Woodman, eds. (Greenwich, CT: JAI, 1987).

Chapter 6: Step 2: Catch God's Story

1. Andrew Root, *Christopraxis: A Practical Theology of the Cross* (Minneapolis: Fortress, 2014), loc. 1334, Kindle.

2. Leonard Sweet, *Nudge: Awakening Each Other to the God Who's Already There* (Colorado Springs: David C. Cook, 2010).

3. There are a range of theological views on the nature of God's work in the world. Some (often called hyper-Calvinists because they have taken some of John Calvin's core doctrine of God's election of those who will become Christians and applied it to every area of history) believe that God causes everything to happen that happens. On the other extreme are deists who believe that people cause everything that happens during this epoch of history until God chooses to intervene and usher in the final judgment. In between are a range of perspectives in response to the questions, "What does God cause?" and "What do people cause?" For a more detailed discussion of these perspectives and their biblical and theological bases, see Stanley N. Gundry, series ed., and Dennis W. Jowers, gen. ed., *Four Views on Divine Providence* (Grand Rapids: Zondervan, 2011) and Terrence Tiessen, *Providence and Prayer: How Does God Work in the World?* (Downers Grove, IL: IVP Academic, 2000).

4. This is the core thesis of Kenneth Archer, *A Pentecostal Hermeneutic: Scripture, Spirit, and Community* (Cleveland, TN: CPT Press, 2009), and summarized in Melissa L. Archer, *'I was in the Spirit on the Lord's Day': A Pentecostal Engagement with Worship in the Apocalypse* (Cleveland, TN: CPT Press, 2015), 45–54.

5. Amos Yong, *Renewing Christian Theology: Systematics for a Global Christianity* (Grand Rapids: Baker, 2014), 336.

6. Mark Strauss, *How to Read the Bible in Changing Times: Understanding and Applying God's Word Today* (Grand Rapids: Baker, 2011), 101.

7. Yong, *Christian Theology*, 342–55.

8. Kenneth Archer, "Pentecostal Hermeneutics and the Society for Pentecostal Studies," *Pneuma 37* (2015): 331.

9. Kenneth J. Archer, *A Pentecostal Hermeneutic: Spirit, Scripture, and Community* (Cleveland, TN: CPT Press, 2002), 226–33.

10. T. M. Lurhmann, *When God Talks Back* (New York: Vintage, 2012), provides an in-depth academic anthropological qualitative study on a specific Vineyard church as well as a historical analysis on the charismatic movement's expectation of being able to hear from God. "At the Vineyard people speak about recognizing God's 'voice.' They talk about things God has 'said' to them about very specific topics. . . . [They] must develop the ability to recognize thoughts in their own mind which are not their thoughts, but God's" (p. 39). Interestingly, at the time of the study, Lurhmann was careful to point out that she was not a person of such faith herself (xxvii–xxxiv).

11. Dallas Willard, *In Search of Guidance* (Ventura, CA: Regal, 1984), 14.

12. Bill Hybels, *The Power of a Whisper: Hearing God. Having the Guts to Respond* (Grand Rapids: Zondervan, 2010), 64.

13. Mark Batterson, *Whisper: How to Hear the Voice of God* (New York: Multnomah, 2017), 14.

14. Choco De Jesus, *Move into More: The Limitless Surprises of a Faithful God* (Grand Rapids: Zondervan, 2018), 14–15.

15. Dennis Lum, *The Practice of Prophecy* (Eugene, OR; Wipf & Stock, 2018) 128–30.

16. Lum, *Prophecy*, 230–31.

17. Lum, *Prophecy*, 229.

18. F. Brown, S. Driver, and C. Briggs, *The Brown-Driver-Briggs Hebrew and English Lexicon* (Peabody, MS: Hendrickson, 2001), 672.

19. Steve Taylor and Peter Furler, "Spirit Thing" (song), *Newsboys: Going Public*, 1994.

20. For example, Acts 16:6–7 describes how Paul and his traveling companions, led by the Spirit, "[had] been kept . . . from" and were

"not allow[ed]" to go to certain destinations, and the Spirit did not provide clear positive alternatives. Galatians 5:16–25 calls believers to "walk by the Spirit" and be "led by the Spirit" with peace being a fruit of the Spirit when we live this way.

21. The Greek word translated "peace" here is *anesin*, which means "rest."
22. Root, *Christopraxis*, xiv.
23. Leonard Sweet and Frank Viola, *Jesus Speaks* (Nashville: W, 2016), xiv.
24. Sweet and Viola, *Jesus Speaks*, 137–60.
25. Sweet and Viola, *Jesus Speaks*, 167–82.
26. Sweet and Viola, *Jesus Speaks*, 161–66.
27. Sweet and Viola, *Jesus Speaks*, 169.
28. Loren Cunningham, *Is That Really You, God?: Hearing the Voice of God* (Seattle: YWAM, 2001), 115.
29. Cunningham, *Really You, God?*, 163.
30. Willard, *Hearing God*, 104–8.
31. Willard, *Hearing God*, 196–99, draws these from Bob Mumford, *Take Another Look at Guidance: Discerning the Will of God* (Plainfield, NJ: Logos International, 1971), and G. Campbell Morgan, *God's Perfect Will* (Grand Rapids: Baker, 1980).
32. Willard, *Hearing God*, 200.
33. Hybels, *Power of a Whisper*, 267–69.
34. Sam Storms, *Practicing the Power*, 97–98.
35. Batterson, *Whisper*, 89.
36. Daniel McNaughton and Bryan Kock, *Follow: Learning to Follow Jesus, 2nd ed.* (Spring City, PA: Morning Joy Media, 2016), 58.
37. Yong, *Christian Theology*, 354.
38. Sam Storms, *Beginner's Guide to Spiritual Gifts, 2nd ed.* (Minneapolis: Bethany House, 2013), 130.
39. Gerhard Kittel and Gerhard Friedrich, "Sofia," *Theological Dictionary of the New Testament* (Grand Rapids: Eerdmans, 1964).

Chapter 7: Step 3: Craft a New Story

1. Mark Batterson shared this during a master's course at Southeastern University, Lakeland, Florida, September 26, 2018.
2. Jim Collins, *Good to Great: Why Some Companies Make the Leap and Others Don't* (New York: HarperBusiness, 2001).

3. Bill Hybels, *Courageous Leadership* (New York: HarperCollins, 2002), 123–27.

4. Ed Catmull and Amy Wallace, *Creativity, Inc.: Overcoming the Unseen Forces That Stand in the Way of True Inspiration* (New York: Random House, 2014).

5. Chip Heath and Dan Heath, *Decisive: How to Make Better Choices in Life and Work* (New York: Random House, 2013).

6. Kounlos and Beeman, *Eureka Factor*, 37.

7. Alex Faickney Osborne, *Applied Imagination* (New York: Charles Scribner's Sons, 1953).

8. For example, B. A. Nijstad, W. Stroebe, and H. F. M. Lodewijkx, "Production Blocking and Idea Generation: Does Blocking Interfere with Cognitive Processes?" *Journal of Experimental Social Psychology* 39 (2003): 531–48; M. Diehl and W. Stroebe, "Productivity Loss in Brainstorming Groups: Toward the Solution of a Riddle," *Journal of Personality and Social Psychology* 53 (1987): 497–509; and B. Mullen, C. Johnson, and E. Salas, "Productivity Loss in Brainstorming Groups: A Meta-Analytic Integration," *Basic and Applied Social Psychology* 12 (1991): 3–23.

9. Nicholas W. Kohn and Stephen M. Smith, "Collaborative Fixation: Effects of Others' Ideas on Brainstorming," *Applied Cognitive Psychology* 25, no. 2 (May/June 2011): 359–71; and S. M. Smith and S. E. Blankenship, "Incubation and the Persistence of Fixation in Problem Solving," *American Journal of Psychology* 104 (1991): 61–87.

10. Nicholas Michinov, Eric Jarnet, Natacha Metayer, and Benjamin Le Henaff, "The Eyes of Creativity: Impact of Social Comparison and Individual Creativity on Performance and Attention to Others' Ideas During Electronic Brainstorming," *Computers in Human Behavior* 42 (2015): 57–67; and Saonee Sarker, Suprateek Sarker, Sutirtha Chatterjee, and Joseph S. Valacich, "Media Effects on Group Collaboration: An Emprical Examination in an Ethical Decision-Making Context," *Decision Sciences* 41 (2010): 887–931.

11. Marcela Litcanu, Octavian Prostean, Cosmin Oros, and Alin Vasile Mnerie, "Brain-Writing versus Brainstorming: A Case Study for Power Engineering," *Procedia—Social and Behavioral Sciences* 191 (2015): 387–90.

12. Shane Snow, *Smartcuts: How Hackers, Innovators, and Icons Accelerate Success* (New York: HarperBusiness, 2014).

13. Edward De Bono, *Six Thinking Hats* (New York: Back Bay Books, 1999).

14. Malphurs, *Strategic Planning*, 46–47.

15. Kristin Diehl and Cait Poynor, "Great Expectations?! Assortment Size, Expectations, and Satisfaction," *Journal of Marketing Research* 47, no. 2 (April 2010): 312–22; Ryan Hamilton, Kathleen D. Vos, Anne-Laure Seller, and Tom Meyvis, "Being of Two Minds: Switching Mindsets Exhausts Self-Regulatory Resources," *Organizational Behavior and Decision Processes* 115, no. 1 (May 2011): 13–24.

16. Luc de Brabandere and Alan Iny, *Thinking in New Boxes* (New York: Random House, 2013), 6.

17. See Thomas Friedman, *Thank You for Being Late* (New York: Farrar, Straus & Giroux, 2018); and Noah Yuval Harrari, *Homo Deus* (New York: HarperCollins, 2017) on how big data is impacting our world in dramatic ways.

18. Heath and Heath, *Decisive*, 11–15.

19. Paul D. Leedy and Jeanne Ellis Ormrod, *Practical Research: Planning and Design* (Boston: Pearson, 2016), 80–82.

20. Heath and Heath, *Decisive*, 80.

21. Kahneman, *Thinking*, 175–84.

22. Snow, *Smartcuts*, 101–22.

23. Heath and Heath, *Decisive*, 202–17; Annie Duke, *Thinking in Bets* (New York: Portfolio, 2018), 218–26.

24. Andy Stanley, *Next Generation Leader* (Sisters, OR: Multnomah, 2003), 52.

25. J. Robert Baum and Stefan Wally, "Strategic Decision Speed and Firm Performance," *Strategic Management Journal* 24, no. 11 (2003): 1107–29.

26. Andy Stanley, "Imposter Shepherds" (speech given at the Catalyst Conference, Duluth, GA, October 4, 2018).

27. Herbert A. Simon, *Administrative Behavior, 4th ed.* (New York: Free Press, 1997), 118–20.

28. Alexander Chernev, "Product Assortment and Individual

Decision Processes," *Journal of Personality and Social Psychology* 85, no. 1 (2003): 151–62.

29. Ali Intezari and David J. Pauleen, "Conceptualizing Wise Management Decision-Making: A Grounded Theory Approach," *Decision Sciences* 40, no. 2 (April 2018): 335.

30. See Joshua, chapter 9.

Chapter 8: Step 4: Tell the New Story

1. Lyn Corno, "The Best-Laid Plans: Modern Conceptions of Volition and Educational Research," *Educational Researcher* 22, no. 2 (March 1993): 14–22 initiates this idea known as the Rubicon Model of Action Phases.

2. Snow, *Smartcuts*, 157–60.

3. Simon Sinek, *Start with Why: How Great Leaders Inspire Everyone to Take Action* (New York: Portfolio, 2009).

4. All definitions in this section are adapted from Gerhard Kittle and Gerhard Friedrich, *Theological Dictionary of the New Testament* (Grand Rapids: Eerdmans, 1964).

5. Snow, *Smartcuts*, 53–77.

6. Brabandere and Iny, *Thinking*, 187–215.

7. James M. Kouzes and Barry Z. Posner, *Encouraging the Heart* (San Francisco: Jossey Bass, 2003), 89–128; and Kotter, *Leading Change*, 121–36.

8. John Doerr, *Measure What Matters* (New York: Portfolio/ Penguin, 2018), 186.

Chapter 10: Shaping Our Story: Making Organizational Decisions

1. Rutland tells his version of his coming to Southeastern in his book *Relaunch: How to Stage an Organizational Comeback* (Colorado Springs: David C. Cook, 2013), 41–45 and 91–93.

2. Kent Ingle, *Framework Leadership* (Springfield, MO: Salubris, 2017), 26–27.

3. Acts 20–21 describes Paul's return journey to Jerusalem. 2 Corinthians was written during that journey and chapters 8–9 describe Paul collecting an offering from predominantly Gentile

churches to meet the urgent financial needs of the predominantly Jewish church in Jerusalem. The list of those accompanying Paul in Acts 20:4 shows representatives from each of the churches sending the offering. This was likely to assure it reached its destination and to build unity with those in Jerusalem.

Chapter 11: Getting Stories Straight: Resolving Conflict

1. David Olson, professor of family psychology at the University of Minnesota, developed a similar system he integrated into his Prepare-Enrich pre- and post-marriage counseling curriculum in the 1980s. It is described in his *Marriage and Families: Intimacy, Diversity, and Strengths, 8th ed.* (New York: McGraw Hill, 2014), 153–56. The version here is unique and adapts new principles based on Story Shaping.
2. Stephen R. Covey, *The Seven Habits of Highly Effective People: Powerful Lessons in Personal Change. 25th anniversary ed.* (New York: Simon & Schuster, 2013), 215–46.

Chapter 12: Epilogue: What's Your Story?

1. C. S. Lewis, *The Last Battle* (New York: Harper Trophy, 1956), 228.

BIBLIOGRAPHY

Archer, Kenneth J. *A Pentecostal Hermeneutic: Spirit, Scripture, and Community*. Cleveland, TN: CPT, 2009.

———. "Pentecostal Hermeneutics and the Society for Pentecostal Studies: Reading and Hearing in One Spirit and One Accord," *Pneuma* 37 (2015): 317–39.

Archer, Kenneth J., and Aaron Gabriel Ross. "The Bible in Pentecostal Tradition." *Your Word Is Truth: The Bible in Ten Christian Traditions*. Geneva, Switzerland: WCC Publications and United Bible Societies, 2018.

Archer, Melissa L. *'I was in the Spirit on the Lord's Day': A Pentecostal Engagement with Worship in the Apocalypse*. Cleveland, TN: CPT, 2014.

Barna, George, and David Kinnaman. *Churchless: Understanding Today's Unchurched and How to Connect with Them*. Carol Stream, IL: Tyndale Momentum, 2014.

Barth, Karl, *Church Dogmatics, Volume I:1, The Doctrine of the Word of God*. Edinburgh: T&T Clark, 1960.

———. *Church Dogmatics, Volume I:2, The Outpouring of the Holy Spirit*. Edinburgh: T&T Clark, 1960.

Batterson, Mark. *Whisper: How to Hear the Voice of God*. New York: Multnomah, 2017.

Baum, J. Robert, and Stefan Wally, "Strategic Decision Speed and Firm Performance," *Strategic Management Journal* 24:11 (2003): 1107–29.

Beck, Don, and Christopher Cowan, *Spiral Dynamics: Mastering Values, Leadership and Change.* New York: Blackwell Business, 1996.

Bloom, Paul. *Just Babies.* New York: Crown, 2013.

Brabandere, Luc de, and Alan Iny. *Thinking in New Boxes.* New York: Random House, 2013.

Branson, Mark Lau. *Memories, Hopes, and Conversations: Appreciative Inquiry, Missional Engagement, and Congregational Change. 2nd ed.* Lanham, MD: Rowman and Littlefield, 2016.

Branson, Mark Lau, and Juan F. Martinez. *Churches, Cultures, and Leadership: A Practical Theology of Congregations and Ethnicities.* Downers Grove, IL: IVP Academic, 2011.

Browning, Don S. *A Fundamental Practical Theology.* Minneapolis: Fortress, 1991.

Brooks, David. *The Road to Character.* New York: Random House, 2015.

Brown, F., S. Driver, and C. Briggs. *The Brown-Driver-Briggs Hebrew and English Lexicon.* Peabody, MS: Hendrickson, 2001.

Cahalan, Kathleen A., and Gordon Mikoski. *Opening the Field of Practical Theology: An Introduction.* Lanham, MD: Rowman and Littlefield, 2014.

Calzo, Jerel P., and Monique Ward. "Media Exposure and Viewers' Attitudes Toward Homosexuality: Evidence for Mainstreaming or Resonance?" *Journal of Broadcasting & Electronic Media* (2009): 280–99.

Cartledge, Mark. *Testimony in the Spirit: Rescripting Ordinary Pentecostal Theology.* London, UK: Routledge, 2017.

Catmull, Ed, and Amy Wallace. *Creativity, Inc.: Overcoming the Unseen Forces That Stand in the Way of True Inspiration.* New York: Random House, 2014.

Chamberlain, Shannon. "Adam Smith and the Romance Novel." *The Atlantic,* September 3, 2014.

Chernev, Alexander. "Product Assortment and Individual Decision Processes." *Journal of Personality and Social Psychology* 85, no. 1 (2003): 151–62.

Collins, Jim. *Good to Great: Why Some Companies Make the Leap and Others Don't.* New York: HarperBusiness, 2001.

Cooperider, David, and Suresh Srivastra. "Appreciative Inquiry into Organizational Life," *Research in Organizational Change and Development.* vol. 1. W. A. Pasmore and R. W. Woodman, eds. Greenwich, CT: JAI, 1987.

Corno, Lyn. "The Best-Laid Plans: Modern Conceptions of Volition and Educational Research." *Educational Researcher* 22, no. 2 (March 1993): 14–22.

Cottin, Jerome. "The Evolution of Practical Theology in French-Speaking Europe." *International Journal of Practical Theology* 17, no. 1 (2013: 33.

Coulter, Dale M. "On Traditions, Local Traditions, and Discernment." *Pneuma* 36 (2014): 1–3.

Covey, Stephen R. *The Seven Habits of Highly Effective People: Powerful Lessons in Personal Change. 25th anniversary ed.* New York: Simon & Schuster, 2013.

Coyle, Daniel. *The Talent Code: Greatness Isn't Born. It's Grown. Here's How.* New York: Bantam, 2009.

Crawford, Matthew B. *The World Beyond Your Head: On Becoming an Individual in an Age of Distraction.* New York: Farrar, Straus & Giroux, 2015.

Cunningham, Loren. *Is that Really You, God?: Hearing the Voice of God.* Seattle, WA: YWAM, 2001.

De Bono, Edward. *Six Thinking Hats*. New York: Back Bay Books, 1999.

De Jesus, Choco. *Move into More: The Limitless Surprises of a Faithful God*. Grand Rapids: Zondervan, 2018.

DeYoung, Kevin. *Just Do Something: A Liberating Approach to Finding God's Will*. Chicago: Moody, 2009.

———. *Taking God at His Word: Why the Bible Is Knowable, Necessary, and Enough, and What That Means for You and Me*. Wheaton, IL: Crossway, 2014.

Diehl, Kristin, and Cait Poynor. "Great Expectations?! Assortment Size, Expectations, and Satisfaction." *Journal of Marketing Research* 47, no. 2 (April 2010): 312–22.

Diehl, M., and W. Stroebe. "Productivity Loss in Brainstorming Groups: Toward the Solution of a Riddle." *Journal of Personality and Social Psychology* 53 (1987): 497–509.

DiSalvo, David. *Brain Changer: How Harnessing Your Brain's Power to Adapt Can Change Your Life*. Dallas: BenBella, 2013.

Doerr, John. *Measure What Matters: How Google, Bono, and the Gates Foundation Rock the World with OKRs*. New York: Portfolio, Penguin, 2018.

Duke, Annie. *Thinking in Bets: Making Smarter Decisions When You Don't Have All the Facts*. New York: Portfolio, 2018.

Dweck, Carol. *Mindset: The New Psychology of Success*. New York: Random House, 2006.

Evans, J. S. B. T. "Spot the Difference: Distinguishing Between Two Kinds of Processing." *Mind & Society* 11, no.1 (2012): 121–31.

Fee, Gordon, and Douglas Stuart. *How to Read the Bible for All Its Worth*. Grand Rapids: Zondervan, 2003.

Finnie, Kellsye M. *William Carey: Missionary Pioneer*. Fort Washington, PA: Christian Literature Crusade, 1986.

Freeman, Emily P. *The Next Right Thing: A Simple, Soulful Practice for Making Life Decisions*. Grand Rapids: Revell, 2019.

Friedman, Thomas. *Thank You for Being Late: An Optimist's Guide to Thriving in the Age of Accelerations*. New York: Farrar, Straus & Giroux, 2018.

Friesen, Garry, and J. Robin Maxson. *Decision Making and the Will of God: A Biblical Alternative to the Traditional View*. Portland, OR: Multnomah, 1980.

Frodsham, Stanley, *Spirit Filled, Led, and Taught*. Springfield, MO: Gospel, 1952.

Gallupe, B. R., L. M. Bastianutti, and W. H. Cooper. "Unblocking Brainstorms." *Journal of Applied Psychology* 76 (1991): 137–42.

Garrison, Alton. *A Spirit Empowered Church: An Acts 2 Ministry Model*. Springfield, MO: Influence Resources, 2015.

Gauntlett, David. *Media, Gender, and Identity: An Introduction*. New York: Routledge, 2008.

Gerkin, Charles V. *The Living Human Document: Revision Pastoral Counseling in a Hermeneutical Mode*. Nashville: Abingdon, 1984.

Gladwell, Malcolm. *Outliers: The Story of Success*. New York: Little, Brown and Company, 2008.

Goleman, Daniel. *Working with Emotional Intelligence*. New York: Bantam, 1998.

Graham, Elaine. *Transforming Practice: Pastoral Theology in an Age of Uncertainty*. Eugene, OR: Wipf & Stock, 2002.

Gundry, Stanley N., series ed., and Dennis W. Jowers, gen. ed. *Four Views on Divine Providence*. Grand Rapids: Zondervan, 2011.

Haidt, Joanthan. *The Happiness Hypothesis: Finding Modern Truth in Ancient Wisdom*. New York: Basic, 2006.

Hamilton, Ryan, Kathleen D. Vos, Anne-Laure Seller, and Tom Meyvis. "Being of Two Minds: Switching Mindsets Exhausts

Self-Regulatory Resources." *Organizational Behavior and Decision Processes* 115, no. 1 (May 2011): 13–24.

Harrari, Noah Yuval. *Homo Deus: A Brief History of Tomorrow*. New York: HarperCollins, 2017.

Hauerwas, Stanley. *The Peaceable Kingdom: A Primer in Christian Ethics*. Notre Dame, IN: Notre Dame University Press, 1983.

Heath, Chip, and Dan Heath. *Decisive: How to Make Better Choices in Life and Work*. New York: Random House, 2013.

Henry, Carl. *God, Revelation, and Authority, Volume II: God Who Speaks and Shows*. Waco: Word, 1976.

Hertz, Noreena. *Eyes Wide Open: How to Make Smart Decisions in a Confusing World*. New York: HarperCollins, 2013.

Hybels, Bill. *Courageous Leadership*. New York: HarperCollins, 2002.

———. *The Power of a Whisper: Hearing God. Having the Guts to Respond*. Grand Rapids: Zondervan, 2010.

Ingle, Kent. *Framework Leadership: Position Yourself for Transformational Change*. Springfield, MO: Salubris Resources, 2017.

Intezari, Ali, and David J. Pauleen. "Conceptualizing Wise Management Decision-Making: A Grounded Theory Approach." *Decision Sciences* 40, no. 2 (April 2018): 335–400.

James, William. *Principles of Psychology, Vol. 2*. New York: Dover, 1952.

Jansson, D. G., and S. M. Smith. "Design Fixation." *Design Studies* 12 (1991): 3–11.

Jefferson, Thomas. "Letter to Peter Carr, 1787." Quoted in Andrew Lipscomb and Albert Ellery Bergh, eds. *The Writings of Thomas Jefferson. Memorial ed.* Washington, DC: 1903–4.

Johnson, Spencer. *Who Moved My Cheese: An Amazing Way to Deal with Change in Your Work and in Your Life*. New York: G. P. Putnam's Sons, 1998.

Kahneman, Daniel. *Thinking, Fast and Slow*. New York: Farrar, Straus & Giroux, 2011.

Kierkegaard, Soren. *Journals and Papers, Vol. 5*. Bloomington, IN: Indiana University Press, 1978.

Kittel, Gerhard, and Gerhard Friedrich, *Theological Dictionary of the New Testament*. Grand Rapids: Eerdmans, 1964.

Kohn, Nicholas W., and Stephen M. Smith. "Collaborative Fixation: Effects of Others' Ideas on Brainstorming." *Applied Cognitive Psychology* 25, no. 2 (May/June 2011): 359–71.

Kotter, John. *Leading Change*. Boston: Harvard Business School Press, 1996.

Kounlos, John, and Mark Beeman. *The Eureka Factor: Aha Moments, Creative Insight, and the Brain*. New York: Random House, 2015.

Kouzes, James M., and Barry Z. Posner. *Encouraging the Heart*. San Francisco: Jossey Bass, 2003.

Leedy, Paul D., and Jeanne Ellis Ormrod, *Practical Research: Planning and Design*. 11th ed. Boston: Pearson, 2016.

Lehrer, Jonah. *A Book About Love*. New York: Simon & Schuster, 2016.

———. *How We Decide*. New York: Houghton-Mifflin, 2009.

Lennox, John C. *Gunning for God: Why the New Atheists Are Missing the Target*. Oxford: Lion, 2011.

Lewis, C. S. *The Last Battle*. New York: Harper Trophy, 1956.

Luhrman, T. M. *When God Talks Back: Understanding the American Evangelical Relationship with God*. New York: Vintage, 2012.

Lukianoff, Greg, and Jonathan Haidt. *The Coddling of the American Mind: How Good Intentions and Bad Ideas are Setting Up a Generation for Failure*. New York: Penguin, 2018.

Lum, Dennis. *The Practice of Prophecy: An Empirical-Theological Study of Pentecostals in Singapore*. Eugene, OR: Wipf & Stock, 2018.

Malphurs, Aubrey. *Advanced Strategic Planning, 3rd ed.* Grand Rapids: Baker, 2013.

Marshall, I. Howard. *The Acts of the Apostles: An Introduction and Commentary*. Grand Rapids: Eerdmans, 1980.

McNaughton, Daniel, and Bryan Koch. *Follow: Learning to Follow Jesus. 2nd ed.* Spring City, PA: Morning Joy Media, 2016.

Moss, Michael. *Sugar Salt Fat: How the Food Giants Hooked Us.* New York: Random House, 2013.

Mullen, B., C. Johnson, and E. Salas, "Productivity Loss in Brainstorming Groups: A Meta-Analytic Integration." *Basic and Applied Social Psychology* 12 (1991): 3–23.

Newell, Allen, and Herbert A. Simon. *Human Problem Solving*. Englewood Cliffs, NJ: Prentice Hall, 1972.

Niebuhr, H. Richard. *The Meaning of Revelation*. New York: Macmillan, 1946.

Olson, David H. *Marriage and Families: Intimacy, Diversity, and Strengths. 8th ed.* New York: McGraw Hill, 2014.

Osborne, Alex Faickney. *Applied Imagination*. New York: Charles Scribner's Sons, 1953.

Osmer, Richard. *Practical Theology: An Introduction*. Grand Rapids: Eerdmans, 2008.

Parker, Stephen E. *Led By the Spirit: Toward a Practical Theology of Pentecostal Discernment and Decision Making*. Sheffield, England: Sheffield Academic Press, 1996.

Perloff, Richard M. *The Dynamics of Persuasion: Communication and Attitudes in the 21st Century*. Mahwah, NJ: Erlbaum, 2003, 128–42.

Petty, Richard E., Pablo Brinol, and Zakary L. Tormala, "Thought Confidence as a Determinant of Persuasion: The Self-Validation Hypothesis." *Journal of Personality and Social Psychology* 82, no. 5 (2002): 722–41.

Rainer, Thom. "13 Issues for Churches in 2013." http://www.churchleaders.com/pastors/pastor-articles/164787-thom-rainer-13-issues-churches-2013.html.

Root, Andrew. *Christopraxis: A Practical Theology of the Cross.* Minneapolis: Fortress, 2014.

Rutland, Mark. *Relaunch: How to Stage an Organizational Comeback.* Colorado Springs: David C. Cook, 2013.

Simon, Herbert A. *Administrative Behavior. 4th ed.* New York: Free Press, 1997.

Sinek, Simon. *Start with Why: How Great Leaders Inspire Everyone to Take Action.* New York: Portfolio, 2009.

Smith, David I., and James K. A. Smith, eds. *Teaching and Christian Practices.* Grand Rapids: Eerdmans, 2011.

Smith, S. M., and S. E. Blankenship. "Incubation and the Persistence of Fixation in Problem Solving." *American Journal of Psychology* 104 (1991): 61–87.

Snow, Shane. *Smartcuts: How Hackers, Innovators, and Icons Accelerate Success.* New York: HarperBusiness, 2014.

Southerland, Dan. *Transitioning.* Grand Rapids: Zondervan, 2002.

Stanley, Andy. *Next Generation Leader.* Sisters, OR: Multnomah, 2013.

Stetzer, Ed, and Mike Dodson. *Comeback Churches: How 300 Churches Turned Around and Yours Can Too.* Nashville, TN: B & H, 2007.

Stiff, James B., and Paul A. Mongeau. *Persuasive Communication.* New York: Guilford, 2003.

Storms, Sam. *The Beginner's Guide to Spiritual Gifts. 2nd ed.* Minneapolis: Bethany, 2013.

———. *Practicing the Power: Welcoming the Gifts of the Holy Spirit into Your Life.* Grand Rapids: Zondervan, 2017.

Strauss, Mark. *How to Read the Bible in Changing Times: Understanding and Applying God's Word Today.* Grand Rapids: Baker, 2011.

Stronstad, Roger. *The Charismatic Theology of St. Luke.* Peabody, MA: Hendrickson, 1984.

Sweet, Leonard. *Nudge: Awakening Each Other to the God Who's Already There*. Colorado Springs: David C. Cook, 2010.

Sweet, Leonard, and Frank Viola. *Jesus Speaks: Learning to Recognize and Respond to the Lord's Voice*. Nashville: W, 2016.

Tillich, Paul, *Systematic Theology, Volume I: Reason and Revelation, Being and God*. Chicago: University of Chicago Press, 1951.

Wegener, Duane T., and Richard E. Petty. "Understanding the Effects of Mood through the Elaboration Likelihood and Flexible Correction Models. In *Theories of Mood and Cognition: A User's Guide*, edited by Leonard L. Martin and Gerald L. Clare. Mahwah, NJ: Erlbaum, 2001, 177–210.

Willard, Dallas, *In Search of Guidance*. Ventura, CA: Regal, 1984.

Wilson, Mark. *The Spirit Said Go: Lessons in Guidance from Paul's Journeys*. Eugene, OR: Wipf & Stock, 2017.

Wright, N. T. *Paul: A Biography*. New York: HarperOne, 2018.

Yong, Amos. *Renewing Christian Theology: Systematics for a Global Christianity*. Grand Rapids: Baker, 2014.